# Marketing's Role in Economic Development

# Marketing's Role in Economic Development

Allan C. Reddy and David P. Campbell

**QUORUM BOOKS**
Westport, Connecticut
London

**Library of Congress Cataloging-in-Publication Data**

Reddy, Allan C.
    Marketing's role in economic development  /  Allan C. Reddy and
    David P. Campbell.
        p.  cm.
    Includes bibliographical references and index.
    ISBN 0–89930–766–3 (acid-free paper)
    1.  Marketing.  2. Economic development.  3.   Marketing—Developing
    countries.  I.  Campbell, David P.  II. Title.
    HF5415.R3349   1994
    380.1′09172′4—dc20        93–27715

British Library Cataloguing in Publication Data is available.

Library of Congress Catalog Card Number: 93–27715
ISBN: 0–89930–766–3

First published in 1994

Quorum Books, 88 Post Road West, Westport, CT 06881
An imprint of Greenwood Publishing Group, Inc.

Printed in the United States of America

The paper used in this book complies with the
Permanent Paper Standard issued by the National
Information Standards Organization (Z39.48–1984).

10  9  8  7  6  5  4  3  2  1

**Copyright Acknowledgment**

The authors and publisher thank the following for allowing excerpts of "Some
Soviet Lessons" by Wassily Leontief, reprinted with permission of the publisher,
M. E. Sharpe, Inc., 80 Business Park Drive, Armonk, New York 10504 USA, from the
September/October 1990 issue of *Challenge*.

# Contents

# Preface

The relationship between marketing and the economic development process has received little attention and little recognition has been given to marketing's contributions to economic development. This is not a new phenomenon. More than three decades ago, management guru Peter Drucker admonished that marketing is the most neglected area of business, particularly in the economies of developing countries where manufacturing and construction are considered more important than the marketing function. Things have not changed much since then. Never before has the need for effective marketing as a means of achieving economic development been greater than it is now. The need for economic development is universal.

All countries desire economic growth and stability. Rich, poor, and middle-income countries all seek better standards of living and ways to achieve them. Many countries, especially some of the poorer ones, realize that significant short-term sacrifices must be made and are willing to make them. Satisfactory development sometimes can be achieved simply by reorganizing and prioritizing existing goals. Other countries may have to make basic changes in their economic, cultural, and/or political systems. As countries strive for economic development, it is important for them to recognize the significance of marketing to the development process. This understanding will enable them to make better use of marketing knowledge, skills, and techniques available to achieve their economic goals efficiently.

This book attempts to demonstrate how a more rapid and efficient economic development can be made possible through effective marketing even though circumstances differ in different countries. This book has implications to a variety of audiences including scholars, teachers, public policy makers, administrators, businesspeople, and the general public interested in the economic development process. It is specifically written, however, in an effort to reach public-policy audiences in poorer countries seeking economic development.

# Marketing's Role in Economic Development

_____ **1**

# Introduction

This chapter deals with general issues related to marketing and economic development. Marketing and economic development are defined, the significance of marketing to economic development is discussed, and some economic development models are reviewed.

## PERSPECTIVES ON MARKETING

Marketing can be viewed in different ways depending on the purpose or situation. The current definition used by the American Marketing Association is: "Marketing is the process of planning and executing conception, pricing, promotion, and distribution of ideas, goods, and services to create exchanges that satisfy individual and organizational objectives" (Bennett 1988, p. 115). As is evident from that definition, there traditionally has been a greater "micro" than "macro" focus in marketing. That is, the traditional approach has been to examine the role of marketing within the realm of an individual firm rather than in an economy. A macro focus of marketing, on the other hand, examines how marketing affects a country's entire economic system in an effort to determine how the system operates and to determine how efficient and fair the system is (McCarthy 1971, p. 7). Thus, whereas micro-marketing deals primarily with issues internal to the firm (target marketing, development and deployment of marketing mix strategies, etc.), macro-marketing deals with marketing's impact on the socioeconomic conditions of the economy. Micro-marketing efforts are usually concerned with the individual firm's long- or short-term profit maximization through efficient factor procurement, product distribution, and final sale. Macro-marketing issues, on the other hand, include such topics as the aggregate effect of government regulations, policies, and actions; social customs; consumption patterns; and the system-driven micro-marketing decisions of individual firms (Kaynak 1986, p. 30). Only recently have the macro-marketing aspects of marketing begun to receive greater recognition and attention; there are now at least two academic journals dedicated to macro-marketing issues, the *Journal of Macro-Marketing* and the *Journal of Public Policy and Marketing*. In addition, considerable literature has been published in the last decade that specifically addresses the role of marketing in economic development (see for example, Kaynak 1986; Kindra 1984; Dholakia 1984; El-Sherbini 1983; Cundiff 1982; Kinsey 1982).

Firms often experience "macro-micro" dilemmas, situations where what is good for the firm may not be good for the society as a whole. For example, the uncontrolled marketing of dangerous drugs, although possibly very profitable for a firm, is probably harmful to society. Conversely, it may be that what is good for society is not profitable for an individual firm. In such instances, the government may take charge and undertake the activity that it sees as desirable regardless of the impact on individual firms. For instance, the government may choose to maintain low-cost health care clinics.

## PERSPECTIVES ON ECONOMIC DEVELOPMENT

Economic development is sought by all countries: the rich, to maintain and further their high standards of living; the poor, to lower their levels of poverty. The present discussion focuses on relatively poor countries. In today's turbulent environment, achieving economic development is more difficult or presents a more complex problem than ever before. The poor nations substantially outnumber the rich and, with the dissolution of the Soviet Union, there are now more countries in search of and competing for resources for economic development. Often, more developed countries are seen as the only source of those resources. Economic development, usually evidenced by industrialization, is considered a must for the maintenance and improvement of existing standards of living.

Economic growth also brings certain noneconomic benefits. The noneconomic benefits can include such items as improvements in social well-being, better education, better health care, elimination of social inequities, improvements in moral and ethical responsibilities, and reduction of environmental pollution are often considered to be the purpose of economic development. Economic development is important, then, because it means a higher standard of living. It allows the lessening of poverty without confiscatory redistribution of wealth, which is usually unsuccessful in the long term. Development allows build-up of a country's infrastructure facilities such as paved roads, railroads, banking and insurance facilities, transportation services, public warehouses, and so on. Nonetheless, economic development must not be viewed as a cure-all for a country's problems since some serious or even catastrophic problems could be political, social, or originating from outside the country. Lebanon, (former) Yugoslavia, and Iraq are examples of this latter case. Economic development, therefore, must be viewed as a means to economic stability and peace rather than as the end itself.

A country is considered to have reached a higher level of economic development when its per capita income and standard of living are higher than the average. In the modern world, economic development is a desirable target whether or not it can solve all of the economic problems. In fact, growth may even, if not properly managed, cause new problems such as growing pollution, crime, and health care problems.

## CHARACTERISTICS OF ECONOMIC DEVELOPMENT AND GROWTH

This book focuses on economic development rather than economic growth. Economic growth means more output, whereas economic development implies not only more output but also different kinds of output than were previously produced. Implied in economic development are changes in the technical and institutional arrangements by which output is produced and distributed. Economic growth can be seen as a subset of economic development.

Economic growth may result from greater inputs leading to greater output or from more efficient use of the same inputs. Development goes beyond this to include changes in the composition of output and in the relative sizes of the contributions of the various inputs to the productive process. Suppose, by analogy, we were interested in the differences between "growth" and "development" in human beings. Growth involves changes in overall aggregates such as height or weight, whereas development includes changes in functional capacities—physical coordination, learning capacity, or ability to adapt to changing circumstances (Herrick and Kindleberger 1983, p. 21). Although economic development is normally associated with increase in per capita income, it includes social advancement as well. Emphasis on intrinsic and aesthetic values, the existence of (relative) leisure, the elimination of drudgery, and marked reduction in interreligious, interethnic, and intercaste friction are some outcomes envisioned as being within the realm of development (Kindra 1984, p. 1). Interreligious, interethnic, and intercaste frictions may be so deeply woven in the fabric of a culture, however, they are not easily relieved by mere economic development. The "ethnic cleansing" of (former) Yugoslavia is a tragic example.

Economic growth is defined and measured in two related ways. Specifically, economic growth may be defined (1) as the increase in real gross national product (GNP) or net national product (NNP) that occurs over a period of time or (2) as the increase in real GNP or NNP per capita that occurs over time (McConnell and Brue 1990, p. 413). Both definitions are useful. For example, if one is concerned with the questions of military potential or political preeminence, the first definition is more relevant. Per capita output is clearly superior, however, for comparisons of living standards among nations or regions. Although India's GNP is almost 50 percent larger than Switzerland's, the latter's standard of living is over 60 times as great as the former's (McConnell and Brue 1990, p. 413). Economic growth by either definition is usually calculated in terms of annual percentage rates of growth. For example, if real GNP was $200 billion last year and is $210 billion this year, the rate of growth is calculated by subtracting last year's real GNP from this year's real GNP and comparing the difference to last year's real GNP.

Economic development, on the other hand, is generally measured in terms of per capita income. Countries that have a per capita income below $200 are usually considered to be less developed countries (LDCs); those with incomes between $200 and $1000 as newly developed countries; and those with $1,000 and above as developed countries (DCs). Per capita income alone, however, is not an adequate measure. Oil rich nations like Saudi Arabia and Kuwait have higher per capita incomes than rich DCs, yet they often have lower standards of living than the DCs. This apparent discrepancy occurs because per capita income is distorted by the presence of very high incomes received by a small number of inhabitants. Per capita income, then, is often viewed in conjunction with the standard of living because these can be more direct and less sensitive to extremes in income distribution (Herrick and Kindleberger 1983, p. 144). Care must be taken, of course, to select appropriate parameters of standards of living; kilograms of meat consumed, for instance, would be grossly inappropriate in an overwhelmingly vegetarian country such as India (Campbell 1985). Some countries, to make the situation more complex, seem to enjoy higher standards of living than they apparently can afford because incomes produced in the parallel or underground economies in those countries are not reported. Actual incomes often are hidden to avoid very high income taxes. Some LDCs (e.g., Pacific Rim newly industrialized countries [NICs]) have been able to achieve rapid economic growth during the decade of the eighties even though a number of them have not enjoyed much economic development (McConnell and Brue 1990, p. 845).

Since the 1950s, few nations have been content with their economic status quo; instead, they want growth, increased standards of living, and an opportunity for the "good life" (Cateora 1983, p. 314). The world's economies are on the move and, although not all countries are at the same level or have the same rates of development, most are experiencing higher personal incomes and technological progress. There is rising demand for goods and services the world over from the least- to the most-developed country. Continual and rapid changes are so much the rule in today's markets that they cannot be ignored. One must be cautious, however, in trying to draw parallels between countries or cultures.

Consumer behavior, for example, is not the same in all countries, even if the countries appear to be close to each other geographically or culturally. A study of purchase patterns in Europe, for instance, showed two distinct patterns of consumer behavior: consumers in the European Community countries spent more on labor-saving devices, whereas consumers in other European countries showed preference for products associated with leisure-time activities, affluence, or product innovations (Cateora 1983, p. 314). Economic development is a dynamic process wherein changes in social, political, and economic forces bring about improvements in per capita income. These improvements are distributed throughout different strata of the population, and those strata may react differently to the improvements.

## OBSTACLES TO ECONOMIC DEVELOPMENT

There are several obstacles to effective marketing that may exist, especially in a poor or developing economy. Some are

1. Poor Infrastructure
2. Inadequate Aggregate Supply and Demand
3. Poor Savings and Investment
4. Scarcity of Natural Resources
5. The Vicious Circle of Poverty
6. The Debt Crisis
7. Excessive Concern for Short-Term Profit
8. Lack of Entrepreneurial Talent
9. Speculative Tendencies
10. Short Channels of Distribution
11. Low Degree of Market Orientation
12. Regional Integration
13. Trade Deficits
14. Balance of Payment Problems
15. Negative Attitudes toward Marketing
16. Bribery and Corruption

Many of these obstacles are likely to be interrelated.

**Poor Infrastructure**

Infrastructure is a crucial factor that is out of the control of individual firms. Aschaurer (1987, 1988) argues that the productivity slowdown in the United States during the 1970s and 1980s was specifically due to inadequate public investment in the economy's infrastructure. Marketing's full potential cannot be realized without adequate infrastructural facilities. Infrastructure includes activities and constructed physical assets that do or can support the endeavors of a number of industries. A major contributor to the economic development of Japan, Germany, and the NICs of Asia is their extensive infrastructure buildup. Countries must shape their infrastructures to support markets and marketing. Infrastructural facets of particular interest can be grouped as (1) capital investment and (2) financial and commercial service. The capital investments necessary to support production and marketing include such things as serviceable roads, railroads, seaports, communication networks, and energy supplies. The financial and commercial services needed include banks to safeguard funds, means of reliable funds transfer, orderly currency conversion, availability of loans, and a stable currency. General business efficiency is positively affected by the presence of good financial and commercial service infrastructures.

Generally, the less developed a country is, the less adequate its infrastructure tends to be. However, as trade develops, the country's infrastructure might also develop to meet the needs of an expanding economy. There is some question of whether effective marketing increases the pace of infrastructural development or whether an expanded infrastructure leads to more effective marketing. Regardless of this "chicken-and-egg" controversy, it takes a long time to upgrade a country's infrastructure. When infrastructure fails to develop enough to adequately support desired and otherwise possible economic activity, countries begin to lose economic growth momentum. Conditions can develop where a country produces commodities for export but cannot export them because of inadequacies of the infrastructure. For this reason, even NICs must struggle with infrastructural inadequacies. Mexico's rapidly expanding economy, for example, has been severely handicapped by its archaic transport system. While waiting for the infrastructure to develop, companies must learn to cope with the prevailing level of infrastructure and tailor business practices to the environments in which they find themselves. The quality of infrastructure directly affects a country's economic development potential and the ability of an enterprise to engage effectively in business. Without proper transportation facilities, for example, distribution costs can increase, and distribution to certain markets may not even be possible.

The growth of domestic market size through the fusion of smaller markets has been, in some cases, the engine powering the process of development (Kaynak 1986, pp. 16–17). Transport and communication are critical elements in this fusion. In other cases, for example, Japan, commercial revolutions, rather than fusion of domestic markets, lead to industrial development. Whether markets pull development or lag behind it, however, the distribution system cannot be neglected. Storage facilities, in particular, tend to be overlooked. Encouragement is seldom given to middlemen, wholesalers, jobbers, who are too often seen as parasites. This viewpoint can be expected to be held by unsophisticated populations and governments because such observers fail to recognize the value added by middlemen. Product standardization may also be an outlet for energy and resources with a high payout in terms of permitting more effective scales of production and reducing costs of distribution.

The growth process can be led by a widening of the market, which, in turn, may result from increased efficiency in transport or communication. Cheapening of transport fuses markets; it brings additional buyers and sellers into contact, making possible additional transactions. Markets also can grow through an increase in efficiency and income in any one product, which often increases the effective demand for other products. This growth can spread in a cumulative fashion. Even where the growth process is led by efficiency in production, however, the requirements of distribution are inescapable (Herrick and Kindleberger 1983, p. 255).

### Inadequate Aggregate Supply and Demand

Economic development should be viewed from both the supply and demand sides. On the supply side, favorable conditions exist when the quality and quantity of natural resources, the quantity and quality of human resources, the supply or stock of capital goods, and technology can support development. To achieve development, therefore, not only must these four supply factors coexist but also a strong aggregate demand should exist for products and services at the same time. Aggregate demand is influenced by a combination of factors such as the size of the population, purchasing power, and propensity to purchase. When there is a lack of demand, the economy can reverse into no growth, recession, or even depression, as happened during the Great Depression of the 1930s.

## Poor Savings and Investment

In many LDCs, both the saving and investment aspects of capital formation are impeded by formidable obstacles. In the poorest LDCs, savings and investment potential are very low, simply because the population has no money. The absence of a vigorous entrepreneurial class and counterincentives to investment are also serious impediments to capital formation and accumulation. Many LDC savers have chosen to transfer their funds to DCs, where greater safety and/or returns are possible, rather than invest domestically.

## Scarcity of Natural Resources

Scarcities of natural resources and limited possibility of augmenting existing supplies may impose a serious limitation on a nation's capacity to develop. Development cannot take place if there is nothing there to develop.

## The Vicious Circle of Poverty

The vicious circle of poverty brings together many of the obstacles to growth and says in effect that poor countries stay poor because of their poverty. Low incomes inhibit saving and the accumulation of physical and human capital, making it difficult to increase productivity and incomes. Rapid population growth can offset otherwise promising attempts to break this circle.

## The Debt Crisis

By definition, LDCs suffer the most from not having the right kind of development or adequate development. Rising energy prices, declining export prices, currency exchange rate changes, and concerns about LDCs' credit-worthiness combined to create an LDC debt crisis in the early 1980s. External debt problems of LDCs remain serious and continue to inhibit their growth. The LDCs are calling for a New International Economic Order that will give them (1) a greater voice in the policies of international financial institutions, (2) preferential tariff treatment, (3) a greater share of the income derived from contracts and leases negotiated with multinational corporations, (4) improved terms of trade, (5) the cancellation or rescheduling of their external debts, and (6) a larger and automatic inflow of foreign aid.

### Excessive Concern for Short-Term Profit

Undue concern for profit and speculative tendencies retard rapid economic development in many countries (Herrick and Kindleberger 1983, p. 253–254). A number of countries in Europe remained at an essentially mercantilist stage of development for long periods. Markets developed and were traded in. Marketers became focused on the rate of profit per unit sold rather than return on investment (ROI). High profits per unit tended to keep turnover small and were maintained only by limiting competitors' entry to the market. Where it was impossible to limit entry, the combination of free entry and price fixing led to overcapacity and underutilization, the infliction of which beset retail trade particularly in Belgium and France (Herrick and Kindleberger 1983, pp. 253–254).

### Lack of Entrepreneurial Talent

What seemed to be missing from, for instance, France and Belgium was entrepreneurial interest in innovation for the sake of increasing profits. Small businesses ran corner grocery stores in the same fashion they "always did." Merchants achieved some status as businesspeople but grumbled that their living standards did not rise. These countries failed to pass the stage of mercantilism until circa 1955, largely because the patterns of trade had become frozen. This suggests that commercial revolution alone is not enough prelude for economic development.

## Speculative Tendencies

Another form of marketing pathology is speculative fever. In Western Europe and the United States, this has not been a major problem recently, but its occurrence in many other economies has been sharp, notable, and, thankfully, short. In the Middle East and many parts of Latin America, social status is accorded to wealth, but wealth appears to be the result of luck rather than work. A corner on the Alexandria cotton market, a squeeze on wheat, or a relatively small movement in the price of coffee, rubber, sugar, or tin can produce sizable fortunes from trading on organized commodity markets. In Western Europe and the United States, possibly because of the size of those economies and the almost instantaneous dissemination of commodity market information, speculation tends to act as a price-stabilizing mechanism. In those developed markets, a considerable part of speculative interest has attached to corporate securities; the speculative position of the owner of a block of shares can be improved by effective production on the part of the corporation and by effective innovation. The incentive to continuous application of effort diminishes in less developed economies, however, where fortunes can be made far more readily and with less effort through speculative excesses, political connections, interest in horse races, football pools, and the national lottery. A World Bank study on prerevolutionary Cuba, for example, referred to speculative interest in sugar in that country as economic diabetes (Herrick and Kindleberger 1983, p. 254).

## Short Channels of Distribution

Channel lengths in developing economies tend to be shorter than in DCs because in developing economies, communities are largely self-sufficient. Each community consumes what it produces and has very little need for middlemen. Channel length will tend to increase as a country develops economically. On the other hand, in a DC, channel length will decrease as a country develops economically (Sharma and Dominguez 1992, pp. 6–7). A longer channel necessarily involves more transactions and more opportunities for profit and innovation.

### Low Degree of Market Orientation

The economic systems associated with socialist or communist political systems rely on central decision making to allocate scarce resources in order to meet industrial as well as consumer demand. In capitalism, market forces guide decisions. Most economies lie somewhere between these two extremes in "mixed" economies. The degree of market orientation exhibited by a particular economic system can change over time. The French economy, for example, traditionally has been characterized by centralized planning. In recent years, however, it has moved toward greater market orientation. A more radical example is China's establishment of "special industrial zones" to spur production and trade. Although the results of this policy have been mixed, the mere fact of their establishment speaks worlds about China's economic system.

Nations vary in their degrees of free-market orientation, and LDCs tend to be found toward the centrally planned end of the spectrum. Several, however, seem to be evolving rapidly toward greater market orientation. A primary result of these moves toward market orientation is accelerating development. Perhaps more important, however, is that the term "free-market-driven politically-repressive" is oxymoronic. Increased market orientation is likely to result in greater freedom for the population.

### Regional Integration

A striking feature of the world economic system in the last two decades is the trend toward increasing regional integration. The rise of the European Community (EC) is a prime example. Fearing that one result of the EC's integration will be protectionism, non-European foreign firms are setting up manufacturing and marketing facilities in the EC. Parallel development is likely to result from integration in other regions.

### Trade Deficits

International trade is fundamental to economic development, but imports must be paid for. Even some major DCs such as the United States and the United Kingdom are having heavy balance of trade deficit problems, particularly with Japan, West Germany, and the Pacific-Rim-based NICs after having had substantial trade surpluses before. The negative U.S. trade balance is due to a number of factors. One of the major reasons is the fact that fewer than 10 percent of the U.S. firms engage in exporting. In addition, labor costs have typically been higher in the United States than in other nations. A high exchange value of the dollar makes American goods costlier to foreigners, and foreign goods cheaper to Americans—thus encouraging an "import pull." In other words, because foreign goods are less expensive to Americans when the dollar is strong, more of them will tend to be imported in lieu of domestic products (autos, electronics, cameras, etc.). By the same logic, a weaker dollar encourages exports and discourages imports. Although a weaker dollar "keeps jobs at home," it does so by a lowering of the standard of living—a lesser assortment of goods is available for consumption.

LDCs often have major trade deficits. Such deficits cannot continue forever without adversely affecting the country's development and standard of living.

### Balance of Payment Problems

Foreign exchange is required for the operation of a vibrant economy to buy essentials (e.g., oil) and to service foreign debt. The lack of it can cripple an economy. The accounting of all the current economic transactions that takes place between a nation and other nations is the balance of payments. By definition, the balance of payments must balance—it cannot be either a credit or a debit. The merchandise account keeps track of the nation's exports and imports, and it is commonly known as the balance of trade. Within the balance of payments account any given category, such as the balance of trade, can be either positive or negative. A balance of payment problem usually occurs in conjunction with a trade deficit problem. In 1989, the United States imported about $110 billion more than it exported; hence, it had a negative balance of trade. In contrast, in 1988, Japan exported an estimated $95 billion more than it imported. This resulted in a positive balance of trade and allowed Japan to maintain its position as one of the world's leading trading nations.

In the short run, a nation may be able to offset a negative balance of trade by borrowing, using savings, selling of assets, and the like. This is likely to be unhealthy in the long run. The U.S. government's high budget deficit has also been a factor in the American negative balance of trade. The United States supported its budget deficit by borrowing from people in other nations. The borrowing made it possible to maintain high consumption levels. U.S. foreign debt has climbed to over $300 billion, more than three times the amount owed by Brazil, the second largest debtor nation in the world. It is speculated that throughout the 1990s, the United States will most likely run a negative balance of trade and increase its level of foreign debt.

Higher prices may generally act to reduce the level of imports, but many products prove to be price inelastic—volume does not decrease despite price increases (Dahringer and Mühlbacher 1991, pp. 97–103). A price change, then, often has little result. Furthermore, it takes time to increase exports. Business relationships, level of service before and after the sale, product quality, continuity of supply, and many other factors influence the attractiveness of goods on the world market. Another factor contributing to the continuing U.S. negative balance of trade is the fact that firms exporting to the United States may accept a lower profit margin in order to maintain price competition. They take a long-range view of profits, choosing to maintain market share until profit margins increase.

Ultimately, American consumers and industrial buyers like imported goods and are often price insensitive. As long as buyers see imports as a better value, because of perceived quality, styles, or other reasons, the U.S. balance of trade is likely to remain negative.

### Negative Attitudes toward Marketing

Marketing education is virtually absent in most LDCs. People in LDCs, in particular, tend to have unfavorable attitudes toward marketing and middlemen. The middleman is often regarded as the one who follows a dishonorable profession and may be considered as the schemer who profits at the expense of the public. The absence of an entrepreneurial class, the dearth of infrastructure, the saving-investment dilemma, and the presence of social institutions are all obstacles to growth. These factors may suggest the need for government action in initiating the growth process.

However, the corruption and red tape that are quite common to the public sectors of the LDCs suggest the government may be relatively ineffective as an instigator of growth.

### Bribery and Corruption

In most LDCs, bribery and corruption are so rampant that nothing happens without them. Some individuals have learned to be so good at the graft game that they have built huge personal empires based on their ability to oil the wheels of the government. They easily get necessary licenses for profitable businesses and are awarded huge lucrative government contracts. Developing a strong economic base is the last priority for these influential businesspeople. Economic planners will have to find ways to prevent these individuals from ruining the economic structure of the country.

These various factors can seriously inhibit, directly or indirectly, the proper growth of marketing activity. This, in turn, can result in the failure to develop the adequate marketing infrastructure necessary to bring about or support economic development.

## SOME ECONOMIC DEVELOPMENT MODELS

Economic development is important to all nations—from the rich DCs to the poor LDCs. What is marketing's role in development? What model explains development? There is no one role for marketing, nor is there one model for economic development, but the two are inextricably linked. Marketing provides a versatile tool that can be used on many levels and in many situations to promote development. Because it operates in the "real" world and is intimately involved with individual consumers, marketing is not constrained by economic dogma. It can offer practical diagnostic and directive guidelines. Its applicability ranges from the ability to promote profitability in firms to the transforming of values and the provision of stimuli for the development process. The need for marketing is continually increasing as nations develop, start trading globally, and set up their own marketing systems. There are a host of economic development models. A few select ones are discussed here to illustrate the process of economic development and marketing's role in it.

### Rostow's Model

Professor Rostow's economic development model has become a classic model in explaining the stages of growth and how economic development takes place. According to this model, countries can be classified by five stages of growth. These stages are (Rostow 1965) as follows.

*The traditional society.* Here there is a marked absence of systematic application of the methods of modern science and technology. Literacy rate as well as other measures of social well-being are low (e.g., Ethiopia and Haiti).

*Pre-take-off.* Here the conditions for take-off are beginning to formulate in a small but important way. There are developments in transportation, communications, power, education, health, and other public undertakings (e.g., India and Brazil).

*Take-off.* Here agricultural and industrial modernization lead to rapid expansion in these areas. Countries achieve growth patterns that become normal conditions (e.g., Singapore and Hong Kong).

*Drive to maturity.* At this stage the country is ready to produce anything that it wishes to (e.g., Japan and Australia).

*High mass consumption.* Citizens have high discretionary incomes and can afford high standards of living (e.g., the United States and Canada).

Most countries would like to be at least in the comfortable take-off stage for the obvious benefits of better standards of living and higher incomes. Only a few nations are fortunate enough to be in the last phase of high mass consumption. Even these nations must continue to recognize and practice marketing with utmost regard. Otherwise, their economic development may be short-lived. Regardless of the growth stages, another indicator of economic development is the extent of infrastructure development within an economy.

### Dholakia's Models

Nikilesh Dholakia (Kindra 1984, pp. 14–15) suggested three models:

*The miracle export model.* To implement this model, the country selects one category of product to specialize in. This is a popular approach successfully adopted by South Korea, Taiwan, Singapore, Hong Kong, and Sri Lanka. Other countries try to emulate the strategy of the successful efforts to become export oriented as these countries have. The major advantages of this model are that countries successfully implementing it experience rapid export growth, heavy investment by multinational corporations (MNCs), and rapid transfer of technology from high-wage countries. Major disadvantages of this model are that it could lead to high dependency on DCs and might lead to a lopsided growth that overemphasizes export-oriented production at the expense of domestic consumer products. Conditions favoring adoption of this model are a sound industrial base and work force, a high potential integration with DC markets, and the existence of authoritarian regimes.

*The autonomous development model.* The basic features of this model are disengagement from the world capitalist system, reliance on appropriate technologies, and collective self-reliance by the Third World countries. Countries such as Cuba, Yugoslavia, and North Korea have tried this model for some time with mixed results. Examples of this model's implementation are Cuba, Yugoslavia, Vietnam, North Korea, and Algeria. Major advantages of this model are autonomous developmental goals, attempts toward balanced development, efforts to achieve "equitable" development, and mutual assistance among similar countries. Major disadvantages are the possibility of isolation from the rest of the world and risk of lagging in modern technology. Conditions that lead to selection of this model are revolutionary regimes, centralized political and economic system, capabilities in appropriate technologies, and widespread education.

*The minor world model.* The countries here try to achieve regional economic power. It is popular in countries such as Brazil, India, and China. Main advantages of this model are relative regional dominance, autonomy, and a fairly diversified economic system. Disadvantages are moderate to high dependency on DCs, the likelihood of geopolitical conflicts, and the likelihood of becoming an industrially and technically second-class country. Conditions that favor this model are large country size with large domestic market, large and diversified industrial base, military strength, and independent scientific and technical capabilities.

Due to the dynamic nature of the economic development process, it is reasonable to expect that countries will have to use a mix of these models, for example, one model for their urban sector and another for their rural sector. Appropriate social and institutional changes and, in particular, the presence of "the will to develop" are essential ingredients in economic development.

## CONCLUSION

Economic development cannot be left to chance. Countries that deliberately plan and aggressively seek new knowledge, skills, and techniques are more likely to succeed in their economic development plans than those who simply wait for the economic miracles to happen. This chapter has reviewed the meaning and implications of the terms marketing and economic development. The relationship between marketing and economic development is examined further in Chapter 2.

# 2

# Marketing and Economic Development

This chapter examines how marketing stimulates economic development.

## THE UNIVERSALITY OF MARKETING'S APPROPRIATENESS

"Marketing is the anticipation, management, and satisfaction of demand through the exchange process" (Evans and Berman 1990, p. 9). This definition is stated here to emphasize two points. The first is that marketing is not limited, as many laymen think, to promoting or selling already existing products but includes all phases of a product's life from original conception of a product through product deletion. The second point of emphasis is that marketing is not limited to the for-profit sector. It exists in all elements of any well-run organization in capitalist, competitive economies but is an appropriate paradigm in all cases that include existing, potential, or latent demand. Some enterprises are better able to anticipate, manage, and satisfy demand than are others. Why? Luck counts, of course, but luck is a poor foundation for any enterprise. Long-term success can only be achieved through effective planning and implementation of marketing management strategies. Marketing strategy deals with the identification of target markets and the markets' needs and the satisfaction of those needs through a combination of marketing mix strategies—product, promotion, price, and place or distribution mix strategies.

### Marketing and Production Functions

Aggressive and sophisticated marketing techniques have been widely adopted in the developed countries. In the noncapitalist and less developed countries, however, marketing is still embryonic if, indeed, it exists at all. The reason for this condition is often primarily political—if marketing activities are permitted at all, they are constrained by the government from being employed efficiently and effectively. Nonetheless, it appears to many observers that certain countries are not yet ready for marketing. We disagree vigorously with this viewpoint. It is more likely that specific marketing activities are not appropriate in certain situations. Which "specific activities" and which "certain situations" are best determined by imaginative and creative individual risk-takers rather than by government edict.

Marketing did not suddenly appear in the developed countries. It developed through an evolutionary process by passing through production, sales, and marketing eras (Evans and Berman 1990, pp. 11–12). The original problem of society was that of production. There was not enough, effectively, of anything. There was demand for almost any product that one could produce. Prosperity for individual firms laid in efficient production. As modern production techniques were developed, demand for some things was satisfied. Firms then had to emphasize their sales efforts to prosper. In the sales era, firms concentrated on selling what they made. Eventually, it was noted that firms that did not concentrate on selling their products but concentrated on making the products their customers wanted prospered more than their competitors. This is the marketing era in which most industries in the developed world find themselves.

Much of the underdeveloped world is still in the first era of industrial development, the production era. There is a perennial shortage of products in a shortage economy; there is unsatisfied demand for almost everything. In such economies, marketing may appear to be secondary to production, and marketing activities may appear to be limited to distributing activities. In other words, physical distribution activities such as getting goods from the production point to the distribution point is more important than demand-generating activities that involve advertising and promotion, marketing research, and so on. It must be remembered, however, that satisfaction of demand is squarely within the scope of marketing. Even if marketing is limited to physical distribution, the interrelated questions of what to distribute, how to distribute, to whom to distribute, when to distribute, and how to notify interested publics in the distribution must still be addressed. Further, as the impoverished economy finally reaches a state in which some demands are satisfied, resources must be deployed in accordance with a coherent plan to take care of other demands. The plan so developed is a strategic marketing plan.

## MARKETING AS AN ENGINE OF ECONOMIC DEVELOPMENT

Marketing plays a vital role as an engine of economic development. One of the ways it plays that role is its fostering of the development of entrepreneurial and managerial skills. In the developed countries (DCs), innovative uses of marketing, appropriate to the situation of each DC, need to be developed to bring economic development to relatively backward regions. The newly industrialized countries (NICs) benefit from using marketing skills as they export their products to DCs and the rest of the world. This is demonstrated by the successes of countries such as South Korea and Taiwan that have achieved rapid economic success and riches—all within a span of a decade (1980–1990).

### Marketing as a Stimulator

Even though marketing plays a vital role in economic development by stimulating demand and taking advantage of the "economic multiplier," it is not always considered important by economic planners. Apparently, less-developed-country (LDC) economic planners traditionally are more production than marketing oriented. They tend to regard marketing or distribution as an inferior economic activity and are more concerned with the problems of production, investment, and finance than with the problems of efficiency of distribution. Furthermore, there appears to be a strongly held, common opinion that an economic system must first have the capacity to produce before consumption and distribution problems are considered. This bias is understandable for two reasons. First, LDC planners often are not familiar with the power of marketing as an engine of growth. This book is an attempt to familiarize them with marketing. Second, planners often have to be concerned with short-term problems. Their people have problems that need solutions *now*. If current problems are so severe that the country cannot care for itself (e.g., Somalia), then outside assistance may be necessary. If, however, a more-or-less stable political situation exists and life-threatening problems have been dealt with, the field is ripe for the longer-term benefits that marketing can offer.

The lack of marketing vitality in developing countries results from misconceptions regarding marketing's nature and applications. It can play a stimulative role in economic and social development by promoting social goals such as birth control, education, investment, and hygiene. Its power must be communicated to students, managers, and bureaucrats. The prevalent image of marketing in these countries, one of a wasteful, parasitic, and socially irrelevant activity, must be corrected with arguments and examples. Marketing skill has played a major role in helping today's leading economies arrive at their current levels of development (Kotler in Kindra 1984, p. xi). It has been three decades since Drucker (1958) and Rostow (1965) wrote articles singling out marketing as a major force for economic change in developing countries.

Among the most important factors in the growth of the U.S. economy have been the large number of "frontier" entrepreneurs and ambitious salespeople, extensive use of advertising media to promote products and services, intelligent use of credit to permit people to buy more than current incomes would allow, and so on. Marketing has techniques to effect changes in the economic development process, yet traditional economists often see marketing as an aspect of production. Rostow's stages of economic growth, for instance, are based on a dynamic theory of production. Such models, which completely ignore marketing as a solution for economic development, are often irrelevant for developing countries.

On the international level, marketing skills are even more central to the development of a country. As a country develops, industrial development depends more and more on performance in global markets. Long-term performance can only be achieved by marketing; protective tariffs and export incentives are only short-term measures. The likely result of protective tariffs can be seen in the case of American industry. Of all the American industries and firms that have benefitted from American protective tariffs, to our knowledge there is only one, Harley-Davidson, that used tariff protection to increase its global competitive strength. All other firms apparently presumed the protection would continue and saw no reason to make better products, cut costs, and so on. In the longer term, only products that meet customers' needs are relevant.

### Marketing Actions and Reactions

Marketing acts both as a catalyst for economic development and a response to it. Because it can play both roles, it is often difficult to determine whether marketing plays a leading or lagging role. Marketing can prove a highly useful tool in inducing rapid economic development.

There are some solid arguments for seeing marketing as a leading activity in development (Bartels 1976):

- Through quality standardization, unified sales promotion, and rational price determination, agricultural markets are extended and production increased.

- Through improvement of storage and transportation facilities, economies in distribution are achieved, markets are expanded, and production is encouraged.

- Through market research and information services, producers better schedule and allocate offerings, realize more stable prices, avoid excess competition, and better serve markets.

- Through product testing, manufacturers determine the acceptability of products, better utilize resources, and avoid waste.

- Through presale packaging, producers mechanize production, distribution, and consumption processes, with resulting economies and efficiencies for all.

- Through strategic location of wholesale and retail establishments, growth of shopping centers, residential areas, and highway systems is affected.

- Through advertising and consumer credit, demand is stimulated, consumption patterns are changed, and markets are opened for the products and new entrepreneurs.

- Through improvement of in-store merchandising, shopping is facilitated and ideas are conveyed for making personal living more convenient and enjoyable.

Another argues (Moyer 1965):

- The marketing system can reduce risks by providing adequate and timely information flows.

- Marketing activity can provide the organizational framework necessary in coordinating production and consumption activities and in rationing the supply of commodities to consumers in response to their expressed needs and wants.

- Marketing institutions can be a source of entrepreneurial talent and capital for other sectors of the economy.

- The marketing system can generate pecuniary and technological internal and external economies for producing firms as a result of the extension of their markets.

- The marketing system may draw subsistence producers into the exchange economy.

- Marketing institutions can increase the elasticities of supply and demand by making available new or improved products that buyers may find desirable.

- Marketing institutions can lower consumer costs by improving distribution efficiency through technological innovation, more intensive resource use, and lessened spoilage.

- The marketing system can reduce transaction and exchange costs between producers and consumers.

Marketing works as a societal change agent. In developed societies, marketing activities coordinate and guide the production, assembly, processing, storage, and distribution of goods and services. This makes marketing an integral part of the social system. The social system moderates the behaviors of market participants as they act within the context of their culture's prevailing values, customs, and traditions. Participants, in turn, affect the social system through their exchange relationships, attitudes toward institutional change, and willingness to adopt new procedures (Kaynak 1982, pp. 3, 6). The development of marketing skills by indigenous managers probably will lag behind if economic development occurs very quickly (Kinsey 1982, p. 68). Shortfalls in this area can be overcome through the activities of multinational corporations (MNCs). Multinational corporations can also be instrumental in maintaining the apparatus for technology transfer to LDCs.

Marketing activities take on increasing importance as a coordinator and stimulator of economic activity as countries become more developed. Marketing is the developer of standards relating to products and services, as well as of standards of conduct, integrity, and reliability. Marketing forces consideration of ethical standards for decisions and actions in dealing with customers, suppliers, the economy, and the society (Drucker 1958). Formation of standards has a direct impact on economic development as their existence reduces the likelihood of conflict and otherwise facilitates efficient operation of system participants. Effective and efficient marketing systems, however, are unlikely to emerge automatically during the development process without a great deal of inefficient "rediscovering of the wheel" (Kaynak 1982, p. 10). An essential aspect of an "underdeveloped" economy and the factor, the absence of which keeps it underdeveloped, is the inability to organize economic efforts and energies; to bring together resources, wants, and capacities; and so to convert a self-limiting static system into creative, self-generating, organic growth. This is what marketing does best.

## DEVELOPED AND LESS DEVELOPED ECONOMIES

The ways marketing is practiced in DCs tends to be quite different from the ways it is practiced in the LDCs. LDC marketing tends to be limited to the traditional roles of promotion and selling; marketing is much richer in DCs. Traditional marketing viewed its function essentially as a linkage between production and consumption. The modern marketing of the DCs, on the other hand, deals with the consumer citizen concept rather than the consumer concept alone. Consumerism, ecology, and relative poverty are common concerns in the DCs (Kaynak 1986, p. 31). All three can have far-reaching impact on the economic development process but they are often seen as irrelevant in the LDCs.

The first and foremost economic concern of DCs is to maintain their standards of living as they maintain the economic momentum they have gained. DCs in the past have tried to cooperate with the LDCs primarily in an effort to develop new markets for the DCs' products. DC firms now are likely to intensify their cooperative efforts with LDCs not only to develop new markets but to exchange the raw materials and other resources that the LDCs have and the DCs need, in return for finished goods, technology transfer, and food. Marketing knowledge could be one of the exchange factors. LDCs can benefit as they gain necessary knowledge and skills. DCs can benefit directly as marketing skills are transferred because they can receive valuable scarce commodities or fuels in return. DCs will benefit indirectly as well as they establish relationships in the LDCs (Kaynak 1986, p. 32).

## ORGANIZATIONAL PHILOSOPHIES

Five alternative philosophies can guide organizations in carrying out their marketing work: production, product, selling, marketing, and societal marketing. Under the production philosophy, consumers favor products that are affordable and available; management's major task, therefore, is to improve production and distribution efficiency and thereby bring down prices. Under the product philosophy, consumers favor quality products that are reasonably priced and little promotional effort, therefore, is required. Under the selling philosophy, consumers will not buy the company's products unless they are stimulated through substantial selling and promotional effort. Under the marketing philosophy, the main task of the company is to determine the needs, wants, and preferences of a target group of customers to deliver the desired satisfactions. Its four principles are market focus, customer orientation, coordinated marketing, and profitability.

Levitt drew a perceptive contrast between the selling and marketing concepts. "Selling focuses on the needs of the seller, marketing on the needs of the buyer. Selling is preoccupied with the seller's need to convert products into cash, marketing with the idea of satisfying the needs of the customer by means of the product and the whole cluster of things associated with creating, delivering and finally consuming" (Levitt 1960, p. 45).

Under the societal marketing concept, the organization's task is to determine the needs, wants, and interests of target markets and to deliver the desired satisfactions more effectively and efficiently than competitors. These activities, however, must be performed in such a way that the customers' and society's long-term satisfaction and well-being are preserved or enhanced. This philosophy demands a balance of company profits, consumer satisfaction, and public interest. Organizational goals and responsibilities can only be considered within the context of long-term outcomes.

## STRUCTURE OF FLOWS IN A MODERN EXCHANGE ECONOMY

Modern economies operate on the principle of division of labor. Each participant, firm or person, specializes in the production of something, receives payment, and makes purchases. Modern economies, thus, abound in markets. Manufacturers buy resources from various markets (raw-materials markets, labor markets, money markets, and so on), turn the resources into goods and services, and sell the products to middlemen who sell them to consumers. The consumers sell their labor for money to pay for needed and desired goods and services. The government buys products from manufacturer and middlemen markets, it pays its suppliers, it taxes the markets (including consumer markets), and it returns needed public services. Thus each nation's economy consist of complex, interacting sets of markets that are linked through the exchange process.

### The Business Sector

The most recent American business groups to take an interest in marketing are professional service providers, such as lawyers, accountants, physicians, and architects. The American Medical Association and American Bar Association, for instance, used to prohibit members from using price competition, client solicitation, and advertising. U.S. court decisions have ruled that these restraints on marketing activities are illegal. Accountants, lawyers, and other professional groups are now advertising and aggressively pricing their services. The U.S. situation is not necessarily paralleled in other economies that always have permitted price competition, client solicitation, and advertising. These freer rules probably ought to be encouraged, because it has been shown that customers benefit from them.

### The Nonprofit Sector

Marketing is becoming increasingly popular in the American nonprofit sector as colleges, hospitals, churches, and performing-arts groups adopt the marketing concept. Over 40 percent of the hospitals now have a marketing director as opposed to only 1 percent a decade ago, and various government agencies are showing interest in using marketing approaches. Social marketing campaigns are designed today to discourage cigarette smoking, alcohol and drug abuses, and unsafe sex practices. Many LDCs have needs for aggressive marketing in many of these same areas plus in a plethora of areas such as family planning and water-efficient farming.

### The International Sector

On the international front, many companies are vigorously restructuring their international markets. Even the communist bloc countries are acknowledging that marketing is good for their economies, especially as those countries convert from their eminently unsuccessful government-controlled to more promising market-driven economies.

## MARKET-ORIENTED STRATEGIC PLANNING

Successful modern companies practice strategic planning with a marketing orientation. Strategic planning involves four planning activities: developing a mission or purpose, identifying strategic business units (SBUs), developing strategies, and implementing and controlling. Some large firms, such as Proctor and Gamble or Coca-Cola, have been able to streamline their planning processes by collapsing a number of products into a few SBUs. Each of these SBUs face specific competitors and each is considered a separate profit center. Several portfolio models, such as those of the Boston Consulting Group and General Electric, are available to help management decide whether the SBUs should be built, maintained, harvested, or divested. Another business activity calls for expanding present businesses and developing new ones to fill the strategic planning gap. The company can identify opportunities by considering intensive growth, integrative growth, and diversified growth strategies.

## CURRENT TRENDS

Marketing in most DCs "is so basic that it cannot be considered a separate function. It is the whole business seen from the point of view of its final result, that is, from the customer's point of view" (Drucker 1973, p. 1). Changes in marketing, such as those noted, are evolving rapidly, and the evolution is itself accelerating. DC customers are sophisticated and unwilling to accept many of the marketing gimmicks of yesterday. Unless the firm delivers a quality product and service, the rest of the marketing effort does not seem to matter. Firms that fail to do so are losing customers and are gradually failing. This pattern seems to be true even for formidable Japanese giants such as Nissan Motors whose U.S. and global market share is slowly eroding. Thus, there is no guarantee that if you were a marketing success, you will always be a success. The dynamics must be understood, and the new concepts should be practiced assiduously.

### Services Marketing

Today about 70 percent of the gross national product (GNP) in the DCs is due to services such as healthcare, education, banking, and insurance (Lovelock 1991, p. 2). Seven out of ten jobs will be in the service industries. In spite of this, ironically, marketing is still taught from the viewpoint of the goods philosophy. Services are intangible, inseparable, variable, and perishable. Each characteristic poses problems and requires strategies. Marketers have to find ways to "tangibilize" the intangible, to increase the productivity of providers who are inseparable from the product, to standardize the quality in the face of variability, and to influence demand movements and supply capacities better in the face of service perishability (Kotler 1991, pp. 470–471). Service industries have typically lagged behind manufacturing firms in adopting and using marketing concepts, but this is now changing, at least in the DCs. There, service marketers are using not only the techniques of external marketing to reach their clients but also those of internal marketing to motivate their employees. Interactive marketing is used to help create skills in the service providers. Again, all of these techniques can and should be used in the LDCs, not only to make the delivery systems more efficient but also to increase the capability of the system to provide more needed services.

## CONCLUSION

Marketing by itself cannot provide miracle solutions to a country's economic development problems. Knowing the power of marketing and making meticulous use of basic and some advanced marketing skills, however, will certainly speed up a country's economic development process. One of marketing's primary strengths is its versatility in the face of turbulence and complexity. Nonetheless, attitudes and present organizational structure complicate straightforward transference of marketing to LDCs. Bribery and corruption, so rampant in the LDCs, can make the application of modern marketing principles and techniques very difficult.

# 3

# Marketing in the Less Developed Countries

This chapter deals with various facets of marketing in the less developed countries (LDCs). These include such factors as the role marketing plays in the LDCs and the likely reasons for LDCs' lagging behind the developed countries (DCs) and newly industrialized countries (NICs) in adopting marketing concepts. The chapter then addresses what actions should be taken.

## THE LDCs

LDCs contain a great percentage of the world's population but a small percentage of its wealth. Countries such as Benin, Burkina Faso, the Central African Republic, Ethiopia, Mauritania, Somalia, and Sudan (all of sub-Sahara Africa) repeatedly experience devastating droughts, civil strife, and on-going corrupt government. These phenomena cause enormous refugee and health problems and make such countries the largest recipients of developed countries' foreign assistance. Their stagnant economies lack almost all the resources necessary for development: capital, infrastructure, trained industrial and agricultural workers, and political stability. To do business in such nations, firms must identify the nations' most urgent needs and develop specific strategies and solutions.

Societies in most LDCs are unaware of the functions of marketing and the significance of those functions. They therefore have doubts about the value of marketing research, marketing middlemen, advertising, and so on. In many societies, marketing middlemen are considered parasites who do not produce anything but make profits at the expense of consumers. In Latin American countries, for instance, the following phenomena were noted by Kaynak (1986, pp. 58–59):

- A serious lack of reliable information about existing marketing systems exists;

- Many public officials and professional workers have definite, strongly held antimiddleman opinions;

- Existing rules and regulations reflect this antimiddleman attitude and serve as barriers to more effective use of resources in the marketing system;

- Political leaders have a pronounced tendency to support physical facility marketing projects such as central wholesale markets, storage facilities, truck terminals, and roads, while giving relatively little support to the development of viable business enterprises and marketing institutions;

- There is a general lack of understanding of the relationships among rural, urban, regional, and national activities related to marketing.

## The Significance of Marketing in LDCs

In the face of increased global competition, LDCs will find it difficult to dispose of their production effectively in either domestic or international markets without effective marketing. The role of marketing in LDCs, then, is more essential and fundamental to development than it is in the developed countries (Kaynak 1982, p. xiii).

In DCs, marketing focuses on satisfying needs and wants in the presence of material wealth. In the LDCs, however, marketing is more focused on delivery of goods and the development of infrastructures to permit further development. Marketers in the DCs must be conscious of societal needs so that they can match their firms' capabilities and tailor their firms' activities to those needs and the capabilities of the countries (Kaynak 1982, p. 21). Today, countries such as India, China, Egypt, and Brazil apparently are recognizing that marketing has a key role to play in the advancement of social programs related to family planning, adult education, hygiene, and the like. Indigenous personnel skilled in the marketing arts are lacking, however. The lack of skilled personnel is being dealt with by some countries. China, for instance, has a long-term agreement with Canada for the transfer of knowledge in various areas, including marketing (Kindra 1984, p. 3). Often the very idea of how marketing can help needs to be communicated to various responsible groups and individuals.

### Sellers' Markets

Most LDCs operate in a sellers' market environment. Because there is a tremendous shortage of all types of goods, anything placed in the market will sell relatively easily as compared to market environments of DCs where more competing firms are selling more substitutes and vying for the consumers' attention. The LDCs' sellers' markets tend to have these characteristics (Kaynak 1982, p. 31):

- Scarce, perhaps rationed, goods.
- Little or no price competition.
- Monopoly or cartel conditions.
- Tied distribution systems.
- Low margins for marketing or profit (the more one sells, the more one loses, especially in a situation of controlled prices).
- Limited nonprice competition.
- Low rate of product change.
- Little opportunity to differentiate products.

### Marketing's Contributions to Development of LDCs

Marketing has the potential to contribute to economic development in a number of ways.

- Marketing can reduce risk by providing adequate information flow from the producer to the final consumer and vice versa. It can provide the organizational framework necessary in coordinating production and consumption and in providing the supply of commodities to consumers in response to their expressed needs and wants.

- It can bring about scale economies due to mass-production activities. Marketing institutions can be a major source of entrepreneurial talent and capital for other sectors of the economy, providing that they are used effectively.

- Marketing institutions can increase the elasticities of supply and demand by making available new or improved products that buyers may find desirable, not only increasing the well-being of people but also contributing to the economic development of the LDCs.

- Marketing institutions can lower the costs of goods to consumers by improving distribution efficiency through technological innovation, more intensive resource use, and minimization of spoilage; this will also improve the overall profitability of firms.

- A marketing system can reduce transaction and exchange costs between producers and consumers.

- Marketing stimulates research and innovation, resulting in new products that can lead to fuller employment, higher income, and a higher standard of living.

## Characteristics of Marketing in the LDCs

Marketing in LDCs is characterized by the following factors:

- Developmental gaps. Throughputs, service levels, institutions, and the like of LDC marketing systems lag behind those of the DCs by substantial factors. Retail outlets, in particular, are physically small with matching revenues.

- Lack of "equity." Needed services and/or goods are not available where needed. There may be, for instance, no ethical drug outlets in entire rural communities and a plethora of them in urban areas. Higher income customers may be charged less than poor customers.

- Nondiversified exports. Exports are primarily concentrated around commodities and raw materials.

- Persistent dualism. Large sectors of the economy remain "non-marketized" in the sense of being outside market systems. When "markets" are interpreted to include social services such as health and education, substantial sections of the LDCs are simply not touched by service delivery systems.

- Monopolistic power. Market concentration and brand dominance are more pronounced in the LDCs than in the DCs.
  Kinship ties dominate among middlemen.

- Dependent structures. Any institution that practices or
  preaches modern marketing is heavily dependent on Western
  counterparts.

Capital shortages and lack of managerial skills and know-how are
often considered to be the major barriers to economic development. Generally, LDCs' marketing problems of today resemble
those that the United States and the Western European countries
had fifty to seventy-five years ago.

The poor countries are riddled with multiple, often interactive,
problems. They have relatively small industrial sectors, are primarily agriculture based, and their exports typically are commodities and raw materials rather than manufactured goods.
Literacy rates are low, while unemployment and population
growth rates are often high. There is usually a shortage of capital
equipment, leading to the use of labor-intensive production methods and low productivity levels. Low real income levels, coupled
with the large family sizes associated with rapid population
growth, cause savings rates to be low. This is often exacerbated by
the flight of capital as citizens try to safeguard their money and
purchasing power from uncertainty created by unstable political
economic circumstances.

Rapid population growth requires high rates of capital formation simply to maintain current per capita supplies. Even when
savings are found to fund domestic capital accumulation, a large
portion likely will be used to supplement inadequate public infrastructure. Private investment is further hampered by the lack of
entrepreneurs willing to take the necessary risks because the perceived benefits are often limited by political and economic instability, low domestic demand for nonagricultural goods, the
difficulties producers face competing in foreign markets, shortages of skilled labor (worsened by the brain drain of trained
workers to DCs), and deficiencies in the existing public infrastructure. Because of these obstacles, per capita supplies of real capital
do not increase rapidly. Low rates of investment in human capital
and the exhaustion of natural resources, often associated with
rapid population growth, contributes to low productivity levels.
The relative abundance of labor also lowers wages. Migration of

labor from rural communities, where there is no possibility of finding employment, to cities, where there is some possibility of finding employment, causes high unemployment rates and concentrated demand for government services in urban areas.

Productivity levels usually can be increased through the adoption of new types of technology, but new methods normally require large amounts of capital and skilled labor—two assets lacking in most LDCs. Furthermore, LDCs' citizens often are not receptive to new production techniques, especially in rural areas. Culture is how we make sense of the world around us; work traditions often are intertwined with basic cultural values. In a hard world, traditional work methods provide a sense of stability and comfort in the short run, even if the methods are dysfunctional in the longer run. Traditional attitudes extend far beyond the sphere of production. Generally, growth in many LDCs is hampered by a series of sociocultural and institutional obstacles whose significance should not be underestimated. Religious beliefs, although possibly offering spiritual comforts to the impoverished, often contribute to rapid population growth and social stratification and, by fostering the so-called "capricious universe" doctrine, discourage accumulative behavior. The lack of institutional and national development can cause widespread corruption, graft evidenced by inefficient and inequitable tax systems, and the possibility of destructive civil discord. Quasi-feudal systems of land ownership provide even further economic disincentives for the mass of rural population.

**WHAT CAN BE DONE**

Today's LDCs can be tomorrow's DCs. The rapid growth of the NICs in the Pacific Rim exemplify a possible future for today's LDCs. The "vicious circle of poverty" can indeed be broken through increasing the rates of savings and capital accumulation. Economic development in the LDCs requires, however, a different set of policies than in the DCs. In order to achieve high rates of economic growth, LDCs must allocate existing resources more efficiently, increase supplies of productive labor and capital, and adopt new types of production methods and marketing. With moderate rates of population growth, this capital accumulation will help increase both labor productivity and output until these countries reach a point where the development process becomes self-sustaining.

Dholakia suggests that LDCs are not at lower "stages" of development, but that they are contemporaneous with the developed world. He argues that LDCs are not forever playing "catch up" with the marketing system of the developed world—even though selected indicators may be interpreted in this way (Dholakia 1984, pp. 10–28). His viewpoint suggests that LDC marketing systems face challenges with problems that will not be resolved by economic growth alone. For instance, the Green Revolution has produced a grain surplus, but up to 10 percent of the output is lost to rodents and spoilage and consumers often spend 50 percent of their income on food. A fully developed system of distribution that efficiently matches consumer needs with production should eventually lower costs and thus the price paid by the consumer—thereby freeing more discretionary income for pursuits such as savings, investment, education, hygiene, and even leisure activities. The development of an efficient distribution system, by necessity, will bring about a more reliable communication system, which, in turn, will facilitate social intercourse and efficient exchange of views among the geographically dispersed channel members. Increased general prosperity, recognized interdependence of population groups, and increased and more efficient communications would encourage interreligious, intercaste, and interethnic frictions to give way to an atmosphere of mutual interest and understanding.

A well-developed macromarketing system also instills a sense of purpose and ethics. Any economy needs standards of ethics and integrity if it is to thrive, but ethics can be seen as an unaffordable luxury in an environment where humanity is too preoccupied with daily existence to worry about "higher" motivations. In many LDCs, it is expected behavior for small businesses—clothing merchants, fruit sellers, or street hawkers—to cheat in relation to quality, quantity, and price of the merchandise. To stop cheating is to stop doing business; Kindra encountered a fishmonger in Sri Lanka who, when found tipping the scales, refused to do business (1984, p. xx). By increasing interdependencies and contributing to the satisfaction of basic needs, marketing can contribute to the formation of senses of business norms and the idea of rightness and wrongness in commercial actions (Kindra 1984, p. 6).

## MARKETING RESEARCH

The function of marketing research in any economy is to provide managers with information so they may make more effective, goal-directed decisions. With that basic idea in mind, marketing research in LDCs has three major roles to play: closing of the gap between production possibilities and demand in the internal market; coordination of activities within the marketing channel; and evaluation of external demand for the country's output, either in the form of exportable products or importables such as tourism. The development of foreign markets must be considered in more sophisticated terms than simply finding ways to export goods and services for which the country has a comparative advantage (Kaynak 1984). For instance, the exporting country must assure itself that exporting of a particular commodity will not have negative long-term effects on that country.

### Problems in Research

There are sociological, psychological, and cultural difficulties and technical complexities involved in the marketing research process in LDCs, but there is no reason to believe the complexities cannot be overcome. First, managers must be convinced that there are benefits to be realized from research. Eventually, managers would likely come to that conclusion but "eventually" will not solve current or near-term problems. Some outside agency (the government, a world trade organization such as the World Bank, or private researchers selling their wares) must make the point to managers, especially to managers of smaller firms. Given the presence of a competent research group and a recognized managerial need, directed research can be undertaken. Managers aware of the marketing environment and the power of information would likely start finding ways and means to initiate marketing studies for the benefit of themselves and, thereby, the economy.

Marketing environment relates to a country's social, economic, technological, competitive, and cultural environment. In every one of these aspects, LDCs differ not only from each other but also

from DCs. The research of firms in DCs is often quite sophisticated, requiring higher orders of skills. In LDCs, however, less
sophisticated efforts may be appropriate. Knowledge of marketing systems in DCs is usually very elementary because the systems themselves are elementary. Research can and must be
undertaken but it will be valued, and therefore encouraged, only
if it yields understandable information usable by unsophisticated
managers operating in an unsophisticated system. Nonetheless,
the skills to perform the research must be acquired either by
training local researchers or by importing skilled researchers.

## THE ROLE OF GOVERNMENT

Government can play any number of roles singly or simultaneously. It can be a planner, facilitator, regulator, and entrepreneur.
As planner, the government must define where the developing
economy should move in the world trade. It may have to provide
seed money for seeking opportunities and to conduct market
research. It may have to spend large sums of money to develop
infrastructure as facilitator. As regulator, the government must
establish rules for fair dealings between businesses and customers, and between businesses. As entrepreneur, the government
must decide on which industries it will focus, which it will own,
and which it will let the private industry run. We suggest that
private risk-takers be given as large a role as possible in making
decisions as to what industries to support and which to abandon.
Governments and politicians, it must be remembered, are political
animals; they make political decisions. There is no reason to assume that they make good business decisions. There have been
any number of politically appropriate and economically disas-
trous projects undertaken by apparently well meaning governments.

Countries are like business firms in certain aspects, particularly
in the management of financial affairs. For instance, although
profit is used as a measure of business success, a nation's surplus
or deficit condition can indicate a country's economic strength.
Countries aspire for balanced budgets at the least, if not surpluses.
Unfortunately, even rich countries like the United States are experiencing chronic budget deficits, while Japan, West Germany, and
the Pacific Rim NICs have become economically strong due to

their export marketing skills and know-how. Japan, West Germany, and now the NICs have mastered the art of low-cost manufacturing and exporting high-quality goods at low prices. Automobiles, machine tools, and the like are exported from Japan and West Germany to the West and other rich nations. South Korean and Taiwanese firms concentrate on exporting computers, steel, small appliances, apparel, shoes, and a wide variety of consumer products.

Invariably, the government has a big role to play in LDCs. Many LDC governments have become more involved in the marketing of basic necessities within their countries, but the policies adopted and the structures and approaches used have reflected many weaknesses and omissions. In India, for instance, government-operated state trading corporations, government-operated milk depots, and other consumer facilities are quite common. Mostly, such government intervention is to enable the common man to purchase meager necessities at reasonable prices. Efficient government-operated facilities are an exception rather than a rule. Government involvement can get quite expensive in all of the areas of marketing mix.

Few players other than government have or can acquire sufficient capital to build the country's infrastructure—railroad, roads, shipyards, airports, and so on. Therefore, the government may feel that it has to get involved in these activities. Here again, however, every effort should be made to encourage private investors, local or foreign, to become involved at every stage of the infrastructural development process. Because private investors are usually putting their own funds into the project, they are vitally concerned with its long-term viability. If investors cannot be found, for instance, to completely underwrite the building and operating of a port, one may assume that the port does not make financial sense. This does not mean that the port ought not be built; it may be absolutely necessary for national defense, for instance. The government would have additional information, investor refusal, and would be less able to mislead itself or its citizens.

Furthermore, LDC governments should simplify themselves at every opportunity. Whatever a government's policies, they should be clear, public, and managed by as few agencies as possible. Great inefficiencies are created by having a number of agencies regulate, for instance, pollution control. As much as possible, a firm should be able to apply to one agency to get all the needed approvals for what it wants to do. Unfortunately, many LDC governments use their agencies as political pay-offs and "make-work" schemes. It would be less expensive for the government and create less overhead for development if the government were to simply relieve its unproductive employees of all responsibilities and send them home. Firms would not have to deal with so many agencies and the government would have a better idea of how much it spends on political and make-work employees. If the funds are available, political-pay-off and make-work white-collar workers could be converted to laborers making actual contributions to their countries by maintaining roads, planting forests, and so on. Bribery and corruption are rampant in the LDCs. Removing unproductive employees will increase the productivity of government and perhaps permit raising the wages of remaining, productive government workers. Increasing wages and providing appropriate supervision are two of the best ways to lessen corruption. Selecting and supporting the right person to deal with firms and economic development may be far more important than the most effective Western marketing techniques (Kinsey 1982, p. 75).

## CONCLUSION

There is no one role for marketing, nor is there one model for economic development, but the two are inextricably linked. Because it deals with the real world, marketing is not constrained by economic dogma but offers practical diagnostic and directive guidelines. Its applicability ranges from the ability to promote profitability in firms to the transforming of values and the provision of a stimulus in the development process. The need for marketing is continually increasing as nations develop, start trading internationally, and set up their own marketing systems.

# 4

# Marketing's Role in the Former Soviet Union and Eastern Europe

This chapter reviews the economic conditions of the former USSR and its allies from a macro-marketing perspective. Strategies to neutralize barriers to affect marketing are discussed.

## THE FORMER SOVIET UNION

The former USSR today is divided into many independent states of the Confederation of Independent States (CIS);[1] Russia is the most dominant. All these countries, together and separately, are going through sea-change metamorphoses from government- to market-controlled economies. It is still early in the process and difficult, if not impossible, to measure the actual degree of progress. Obviously, the members of the CIS are experiencing severe difficulties. There are extreme shortages of goods, prices are soaring, and there is great political turmoil. In spite of, and often because of, this situation certain policy decisions must be made. The need for a greater role for marketing in the CIS's economic development must be recognized and emphasized. Major barriers to effective marketing exist. A macro-marketing perspective offers the best chance to overcome those barriers.

## Transformation to a Free-Market System

Moving to a free-market system is an almost unbelievably radical departure for Russia and the other members of the CIS. Their economies have been centrally managed for more than seventy years, three generations. The change sometimes appears to be an overwhelmingly ambitious undertaking because the government-controlled economies have become part of the culture. The change, nonetheless, is expected to end chronic shortages in food, housing, and other essentials and integrate the CIS into the world market. Decades of tight central control will be reversed. The forces of the marketplace will be unleashed to determine prices, what products to produce, how to produce them and where. Success depends on how well the public and bureaucrats respond to changes that are demanded under the new system. An understanding of the significance of marketing in economic development and viewing the entire process of development from a macro-marketing perspective is critical.

## Marketing Stimulates Economic Development

Marketing stimulates economic development. It can act as a catalyst in that it accelerates the developmental process that helps promote higher standards of living. It can trigger rapid economic growth by stimulating the development of a production-distribution-consumption economy. Drucker pointed out the importance of marketing to economic development three decades ago (1958, p. 252): "[Marketing's] effectiveness as an engine of economic development with special emphasis on its ability to develop rapidly much-needed entrepreneurial and managerial skills needs hardly any elaboration. Because it provides a systematic discipline in a vital area of economic activity it fills one of the greatest needs of a developing economy." The economic success of developed countries and the newly industrialized countries (NICs)—such as Hong Kong, Singapore, South Korea, and Taiwan—demonstrates how marketing plays a paramount role in economic development. As has Japan, the Pacific basin NICs have progressed, through successful export marketing, from relative rags to riches in a short period (Reddy 1989).

## Historical Perspective of the Soviet Economy

Nobel laureate economist Professor Wassily Leontief provides an historical perspective of the USSR (1990).

Following World War I, the [USSR's] economy was in shambles. Manufacturing industry was destroyed, and industrial workers had no goods to exchange for agricultural commodities. Military detachments sent to the countryside by the government confiscated the grain stores held by the farmers and brought them to the cities to supply bread to the starving urban dwellers. The farmers responded, as they always do in such situations, by curtailing output.

Lenin saw that this wasn't working and introduced the so-called "new economic policies" establishing a free market for agricultural commodities—inviting peasants to "enrich themselves." Farmers resumed production, but with industries still in shambles, the cities still couldn't produce the commodities needed to be supplied in exchange for food. The farmers went on strike again. Stalin answered with collectivization, which amounted to taking away the means of production from the farmers and making them pay for their use by surrendering to the government a large part of agricultural product.

The government thus has the power to determine how much to allocate to current consumption. High rates of investment transformed Russia from a relatively backward agricultural country into a great industrial power . . . [and] the Soviet economy grew very fast in the 1950s and 1960s. A large part of the rising output went into investment and maintenance of the military establishment, but the standard of living also rose substantially. All this was achieved by a straight command economy. The system enabled the Soviet union to industrialize rapidly, but it also created all the wrong incentives. People's self-interest was not in producing efficiently, but in manipulating the bureaucracy so as to improve one's situation. Not surprisingly, productivity began to fall and so did the standard of living of the large masses.

Gorbachev realized, as did Lenin before the introduction of the so-called "new economic policies," that it was necessary to mobilize individual economic self interest. Before *perestroika*, black marketers were the only real entrepreneurs in the Soviet Union, and in a sense they contributed much to the economy. . . . Thus, potential entrepreneurs were already present in Russia; to make entrepreneurship contribute to economic efficiency, it is, however, necessary to place at its disposal a viable market mechanism with rational competitive pricing.

Three critical steps have to be taken by the CIS to set their economies right (Leontief 1990, p. 15): fixing the price system, reforming the currency, and instituting fiscal reforms aimed at balancing the budget. He suggests that these three steps must be taken simultaneously rather than one at a time because of the inevitable rapid erosion of living standards under the present chaotic conditions. Under a plan proposed by Gorbachev, the Kremlin would continue to run such strategic economic sectors as energy, banking, defense production, trade, transport, and communications. It is easy to understand why this strategy appealed in some quarters. The USSR was willing to take giant steps to free some industries now but felt that central control was necessary to keep certain industries viable. However, a market economy cannot function well if all its different parts are not aligned properly. Replacing the four tires on a car with tires of different designs, gradually or one at a time, would unbalance the vehicle and likely land it in a ditch. Suddenly shifting to a free-market economy, changing all four tires at once, will be no easy task. As will be seen, the lack of commercial and physical infrastructure and market traditions will greatly impede the transition.

### Switching to Free Markets

Communist nations traditionally have traded more among themselves than with others. Because their trading partners were themselves centrally planned economies, there was little or no concept of competition. There was no need to develop, so development was stifled. Except for a few advances in military and space sciences, the technological level of consumer goods manufacturing in the CIS is at a primitive stage. The production of consumer goods has been dismally low, causing shortages in vital commodities such as food, shelter, and other essentials. Frequent shortages make citizens unhappy and restless about their consistently deteriorating living standards. The fact that the USSR was unable to offer a decent standard of living to its citizens, even though it was a military superpower, demonstrates the utter failure of a government-controlled economy. With the exception of a few upper-class bureaucrats, people could not obtain products taken for granted in the West—cigarettes, meat, and the like. Milton and Ruby Friedman noted that (Friedman and Friedman 1980, p. 137) "Russia is a country of two nations: a small privileged upper-class of bureaucrats. Communist party officials, technicians; and a great mass of people living better than their grandparents did. The upper class has access to special shops, schools, and luxuries of all kinds; the masses are condemned to enjoy little more than the basic necessities." This creation of what is, in effect, a new aristocracy appears to be the inevitable result of communism's strong central government (Djilas 1963). Hayek, in fact, argues convincingly that the natural outcome of any overly strong central government regardless of the economic philosophy or system under which it claims to operate (socialist, communist, fascist, nazi, capitalist, etc.) is the loss of personal freedoms by citizens (1976).

Under the present circumstances, two of the CIS's pressing problems are those of raising capital for developmental purposes and the acquiring of management and marketing skills. Capital is required to set up more efficient, more advanced factories to produce consumer goods; to establish distribution channels; and to create reliable and efficient transportation, storage, and inventory control systems. The acquisition of management and marketing know-how and skills can only hasten economic development. Development is a complex undertaking; it must be managed. That management can best be done by entrepreneurs and risk takers. Unless the capital and management/marketing skills can be acquired from the developed countries, the CIS may have to develop its own indigenous technologies and rely on the development of its own commercial culture. These would take many years to develop. It is unlikely that the political situation in the CIS would permit such a delay; civil war would not be an impossibility.

To solve the first problem, the CIS must permit and encourage foreign capital investment. According to the classical economist Adam Smith, capital must be procured even if it means relinquishing control of a segment of business to foreigners (Smith 1937, p. 360): "The wealth of ancient Egypt, that of China and Indostan [sic], sufficiently demonstrate that a nation may attain a very high degree of opulence, though greater part of its exportation trade be carried on by foreigners." This statement was made over a half century ago, but is as true today as it was then. The second problem, the acquisition of management and marketing know-how and skills, can be solved by allowing and encouraging foreign firms to produce, market, and sell in the CIS market. As modern CIS industries arise, there will undoubtedly arise pressures for protectionism. These pressures must be countered lest the developmental process be arrested.

### The Soviet Market

The Soviet market consisted of an ostensibly simple system in which the government produced and distributed products and services to consumers. The proposed change to a free-market system will not take place all at once. Today, government agencies apparently are being gradually replaced with profit-making private ventures. At the current pace, it will be many years before the economy reaches a level of marketing sophistication where intermediaries compete among themselves to serve as the primary link between producers and consumers.

### Barriers to Marketing

Some of the barriers to marketing and development may be able to be overcome by direct government action. Others, however, are behavioral and attitudinal. They must be overcome by the citizenry with, perhaps, governmental education and assistance. Some of the major barriers are:

*Lack of resources to produce and distribute consumer goods in abundance.* The production of consumer goods has been neglected; military production was emphasized. Even now, major expenditures of scarce resources are being spent on arms. The level of technology used in the consumer goods sector is primitive, causing frequent shortages and a high rate of defective products. In the face of recurring shortages, the citizens react rationally—they hoard either for personal use or in speculation (Summers 1990, p. 16). Vast quantities of products are wasted due to improper storage and warehousing. The ultimate consumer good, food, rots in the field for want of the resources to distribute it.

*Lack of understanding of capitalism.* Capitalism has been the official enemy; those who practiced it have, heretofore, been official criminals. The public and bureaucrats do not appear to understand the risks that must be accepted under capitalism. Capitalism provides the opportunity to prosper but requires that the risk of failure be accepted. Free markets, democracy, free enterprise, profit, risk-taking, and the like cannot operate smoothly and efficiently unless they are understood.

*Lack of political background.* The individuals who are and will be responsible for leading the CIS have no experience in operating in a nonauthoritarian environment.

*Lack of sophisticated infrastructure.* Effective marketing needs appropriate infrastructural support. The infrastructure in the CIS must be sophisticated because of the vast distances, large populations, and crowded urban areas involved. The CIS needs banks, insurance firms, transport networks, the media, and the like capable of supporting major industries and turbulent environmental conditions. These support organizations cannot be formed and become fully operative overnight. An experience base is necessary for development and operation.

*Lack of legal and contractual framework.* Businesses cannot function in a vacuum. Existence of a good legal system is necessary for most business transactions to design and execute contracts between parties, and to safeguard interests from exploitation by others. "Contract" is a basic legal concept in any commercial society. This legal and contractual environment has been totally absent in the USSR. Further, the legal system that did exist was limited primarily to examining crimes against the state (political) and other individuals (criminal) rather than matters related to civil laws. A legal and contractual framework must be developed from the ground up.

*Lack of convertible currency.* Convertibility depends on many things, such as the country's trade balances, internal budget deficits, and how other countries view the currency value. Because commerce in the USSR primarily was with other communist nations and frequently was based on barter, convertibility was not an issue. The CIS, however, can no longer be supported by barter. If foreign firms are to do business there, investing capital and skills, those firms must be paid in some coin. An unconvertible currency is of little use to such an investing firm. Further, a convertible currency is necessary for any but the most trivial international business.

*Lack of business culture appropriate for a market-driven eonomy.* In market-driven economies, both sellers and buyers know their roles, and there is little confusion in initiating or closing business deals. In the CIS, however, individuals probably are unaware of their roles in business transactions. The Soviet antibusiness approach ruled them for three generations; they do not understand what is required of them. The satellites were antibusiness for a shorter period, perhaps, but one and a half generations is a long time. Business needs standards of integrity, honesty, expertise, and quality if it is to expand (Cateora 1990, p. 3). The situation is further complicated by the sometimes horrendous conditions in which CIS citizens live. A population struggling for survival tends to overlook the importance of private ownership of personal property.

*Lack of consumer orientation.* The USSR and its satellites used advertising mainly as a propaganda tool to indoctrinate the population in socialism and communism. The consumer advertising industry, therefore, is in its infancy.

*Lack of market research and demand forecasting mechanisms.* In centrally planned economies, the demand for goods and services is estimated by the central government planners. The government then tries to satisfy demand based on availability of products and services, only after the government has provided the goods and services it needs to satisfy its own goals. Because individual consumption is subject to production in these economies, people learn to live in a seller's economy. Also, most trade has been conducted by various government-owned-and-operated state trading organizations rather than by individual, profit-oriented end-users (Cateora 1990, p. 312). Because there is no need to research the market in centrally planned economies, the mechanisms and skills to do so do not exist. Limited contact with final users and a dearth of available data are common problems (Kahler 1983, p. 360).

Further, individuals are either ignorant of the significance of marketing research or may consider consumer surveys as methods whereby the government tries to collect derogatory information about the citizens. Because of these fears, cooperation from the people in collecting valuable marketing research information would not be expected. Such fears will probably lessen as democracy and citizen-responsive governments take hold but fundamental suspicions about answering questions for strangers have likely been elevated to cultural values. Even if this suspicion is overcome, people will still not be aware of the critical role of marketing research.

*Attitude of dependence on the government and/or the USSR.* Russia has controlled Eastern Europe since World War II and the soviet republics for seventy years. Essentials such as oil, food items, and so forth have been provided or controlled by the USSR. The feeling of independence and responsibility to provide for their own basic needs will be difficult for the newly liberated countries to develop.

*Ability to prosper depends on the perception of the developed democracies.* Much of the initial capital, know-how, and technology has to be imported from the Western countries. With the exception of East Germany where West Germany has quickly stepped into action, it is difficult to predict the fate of the other countries in terms of attracting foreign capital and know-how. Transferring dependence to the United States will not be enough. The United States needs to invest its capital carefully because of its own economic situation.

*Prevailing attitudes of other countries in the region may not be favorable for economic development.* Unified Germany now looks after its own interests first. The European Community (EC) is busy protecting its markets from U.S. and Japanese competitors (Quelch, Buzzell, and Slama 1992). Unless the communist bloc countries mobilize their own strength and accept responsibility for their own futures, it is difficult to expect that other countries will help. To the contrary, other countries might see their own best interests in controlling competition from the less experienced East European countries in the newly expanding markets.

*Multinational corporations (MNCs) may try to prevent the formation and growth of independent east European firms.* MNCs from the United States, Japan, and Europe have vast resources. They can quickly establish subsidiaries and may attempt to prevent the formation and development of independent East European firms. With enormous capital at their disposal, some large MNCs are able to achieve their competitive objectives by political means. MNCs that have mastered the four P's (product, preparation, persistence, and patience) are quickly succeeding in other socialist countries like China (Larson 1988, pp. 79–90). For these MNCs, Eastern Europe is another testing ground. However, this is not to be seen as totally negative yet, particularly in view of the geographic location of East European countries to the EC and the rest of Western Europe, the second largest consumer market in the world.

*Global markets are flooded with goods from developed countries (DCs), less developed countries (LDCs), and* newly industrialized countries *(NICs)*. To generate capital, East European economies need to sell their products to other countries for profit. Global markets, however, are already flooded with numerous goods from the developed countries, less developed countries, and newly industrialized countries.

## RECOMMENDED STRATEGIES

Eastern Europe and the CIS are at the crossroads. Each country must choose a market system to suit its economic objectives. The CIS and its members' economies are enormous; any momentum acquired will be very difficult to redirect. Decisions made now, then, will be extremely difficult to change. It is not enough to say that there will be no going back to the totally ineffective old system; specific actions must be taken to foster the growth of free economies. We recommend the following initial strategies to facilitate and encourage the appropriate changes in public policy and the general attitude of the citizenry. More strategies undoubtedly will evolve as the CIS progresses toward introducing free markets in all business sectors and resolves the growing conflict between the central government and the republics.

### Convertible Currencies

Most convertible currencies are not "backed" by gold or any other precious commodity. The U.S. dollar, for instance, is backed only by the perception, held by currency traders and private firms, that the dollar has value and that the U.S. economy will continue to provide reasonably stable value for the dollar. Currency traders and firms, however, do not perceive the same safety in the currencies of the newly liberated economies. There currencies, then, must be "pegged" to something of perceived value. One possibility is for some developed country to guarantee that it will buy and sell the weak currency at some fixed exchange rate.

For instance, the United States could guarantee to buy and sell the Russian ruble for so many rubles to the dollar. This would make the ruble as convertible as the dollar. Unfortunately, given the current situations of the economies of most of the developed nations, this is probably not financially or politically possible.

A more likely possibility is to peg the weak currency to some commodity of worth. Gold and silver have the most recognition as specie, of course, but there is no technical reason to limit the choices to those two. There are a number of precious and semiprecious materials that could serve as well. Palladium or iridium for instance, could serve. The commodity selected should have three basic attributes: (1) massive discoveries of the commodity are unlikely; (2) quantum technological changes in extraction capabilities are unlikely; and (3) the country must possess stocks, either in hand or in production capacity, of the commodity. Oil, for instance, would subject the currency to the risks of the oil market with its sometimes wild fluctuations. A currency pegged to oil would fluctuate in value with the value of oil.

## Allow Foreign Capital and Entrepreneurs

The CIS is badly in need of modern manufacturing technologies and managerial/marketing skills; importing them from the developed democracies is probably the only way to acquire them quickly. There probably is no more effective strategy to support rapid development of businesses than to allow foreign capital and business free access into the CIS. Restrictions must not be placed on ownership and profit repatriation.

## Cut Defense Expenditures to the Bare Minimum

Because superpower military rivalry has ended, there is no point in maintaining a massive and burdensome military. Some military strength is undoubtedly necessary for national security but, in the absence of a strategic threat, strategic nuclear weaponry and massive conventional capabilities are simply wasteful. If the United Nations assumes its intended role among nations, a goal to which it appears to be struggling, massive military strength in economically weak nations will become still more superfluous.

## Democratize the Nations at the Grassroots Level

The process of democratization must be pervasive from the local to the national levels and everything in between. The old bureaucratic ways of doing things must stop. *Apparatchiks* still in place must step down; accept, support, and implement the new paradigm; or quickly be removed. If they remain positions of authority and keep their "strong-central-government" mindsets, they will likely remain as sources of pressure to return to a command economy and authoritarian central government with potentially catastrophic results.

## Establish Mentor Relationships with Democracies

The newly liberated countries need guidance and help from their counterparts in the democracies. The democracies can train politicians and bureaucrats to run a new, different, and, to them, strange form of government.

## Decentralize International Business

Risk-takers must be permitted to make their own decisions. This most important strategy is being implemented in many of the liberated countries—a growing number of ministries, foreign trade organizations, and individual companies are beginning to do international business on their own. Bulgaria canceled the state monopoly on international trade in 1989. Poland permits each company to establish trade relationships with international partners. By 1990, 900 Polish companies already had their own foreign currency accounts. New Polish legislation permits the foundation of independent commercial banks which can finance themselves under free-market conditions. Hungary has followed a similar path. By 1990, Hungarian companies could import more than 260 goods without licenses, including metal-carving machines, paper, and fish (Dahringer and Mühlbacher 1991, pp. 81–82).

Individual firms are becoming more and more financially responsible for their own performances: the government is no longer liable for their debts. Companies that are not able to eliminate their deficits will be closed. This decentralization still has to go a long way, however, before the economic system is comparable to Western industrialized nations.

## Decontrol Enterprise

The control of a risk-taking enterprise must be in the hands of the risk-takers. The more risk-takers are permitted and encouraged, the more rapidly economic development can occur. Private enterprise is being permitted and often encouraged in some countries, but the enactment of this strategy has been spotty. Bulgaria introduced shareholder companies, which can be completely private or even foreign-owned. In Poland the "Act on Business Activities" legalized private enterprise. Poles have begun to buy formerly public companies. A major barrier to faster development of private initiatives, however, is the lack of management know-how, capital, and a sufficient supply of products. In Hungary, there is a strong tendency to privatize industrial companies, commerce, and restaurants. Private banks were created in 1988. In August 1989, Getz, a U.S. trading company, was the first Western company to own 100 percent of a formerly public Hungarian company, Intercooperation (Dahringer and Mülbacher 1991, pp. 81–82).

## Encourage and Support Joint Ventures

This strategy provides one of the best ways for Eastern European managers to gain the know-how, experience, and financial resources needed to prosper in a market economy. A joint venture is often attractive to a foreign investor because it allows the foreigner to quickly gain footholds in a new country while limiting reduced risk. The foreign firm gains the market knowledge (including culture, language, and other "soft" assets) of its local partner. At the same time, the local partner gains access to financing plus the managerial and marketing skills of its foreign partner. Both partners want the venture to succeed, so both try to provide what its partner needs (Dahringer and Mühlbacher 1991, p. 316). Poland and Hungary have the most advanced legislation regarding joint ventures of all Eastern European countries; there are no restrictions on the percentage of equity held by foreign firms. Hungary has formed "Investcenter," which facilitates contracts between potential Hungarian and foreign joint venture partners. Nearly 400 joint ventures had been formed by early 1990, many of them in services or the construction business, and some of them in manufacturing. Suzuki, for example, will produce 50,000 of its

Swift models in Hungary, while General Motors will produce car engines and Philips had entered the light bulb business (Dahringer and Mühlbacher 1991, pp. 81–82). The Creditanstalt, an Australian bank, founded the first broker house in Eastern Europe with a bank located in Budapest. The London Stock Exchange and New York–based Bear, Stearn & Co. joined forces to help set up a Hungarian stock exchange. Joint venture regulations were liberalized, although not as much, in the other Eastern European nations too.

### Foster Export-Led Development

Exporting has great promise for Eastern Europe, especially as appropriate joint ventures are formed. The exporting may be from the basis of a resource-rich or a resource-poor country or region. Regions of Russia, for instance, are resource-rich. They are blessed with large petroleum reserves. Other regions have mineral deposits, rich farm land that only needs modern techniques and management to be productive, timber, or other natural assets that can be successfully exploited and exported.

Resource-poor areas must learn to produce goods that are in demand. For instance, resource-poor Japan's fantastic economic achievement is completely based on its export strength. Concerted cooperation among government, industry, and the labor force helped to identify and emphasize a series of industries for which demand was great and for which quality of output was important. Contrary to popular belief, superior technology does exist in many of the new liberated countries; they do produce export quality products that can compete in the world markets (Wood and Darling 1993, p. 99). Like Japan, Eastern Europeans must not hesitate to alter their concentrations as economic conditions change. Comparative advantage changes as time proceeds. A country cannot concentrate forever on a given set of products and expect to maintain its developmental momentum; today's "star" may be tomorrow's "dog." Flexibility and agility will be needed. They can best be supplied by risk-takers. The resource-rich and -poor strategies can be complementary. "Resource-rich Korea," for instance, exports skilled construction labor and management to enormous projects all over the world. "Resource-poor Korea" has relatively recently entered into electronics, computers, and automobiles (Herrick and Kindleberger 1983, pp. 428–430).

Any country eager to export manufactured goods must realize that industrial exports are sold in complex combinations of terms and conditions. Total prices reflect elements in the package. For example:

a. Specifications for the goods, including quality. Poor countries' exports must be of high quality to be competitive in world markets.

b. Credit terms. When prices and other specifications are equal, the country whose firms can offer the best credit terms will get the order. This challenges poor countries that are more often the importers of capital than extenders of industrial credit.

c. Delivery dates. Delivery dates for large, lumpy exports (big machinery, ships, aircraft) reflect delivery capability. Questions of delivery reliability must be resolved to the customers' satisfaction.

d. Currency. If countries insist that their export contracts be denominated a "strong" currency, customers will be harder to attract than if weaker currencies are accepted. Some measure of sophistication must be possessed by the exporter to develop appropriate hedges or other currency risk-limiting techniques.


## U.S. TRADE WITH EASTERN EUROPE

Trade with the USSR and its satellites has not been viewed as important to free world foreign trade. The United States, for example, exported less than $1 billion to Eastern Europe in 1988, as shown in Table 4.1, and imported just over $1.5 billion. As a result, very few free-world firms had any presence in the eastern bloc and few, if any, governmental support structures exist. It appears that governmental efforts to encourage trade with the eastern bloc are primarily ad hoc. Given the notable lack of flexibility, agility, and realistic expectations of most government agencies (Campbell 1987), the aid provided by government agencies can be expected to be of the "it is better than nothing" variety. The burden and the opportunity will fall to private firms.

Table 4.1
U.S. Trade with Eastern Europe, China, and Russia, 1988[1]

|  | Exports | Imports |
|---|---|---|
| Eastern Europe | 882 | 1,580 |
| Bulgaria | 127 | 27 |
| Czechoslovakia | 55 | 88 |
| East Germany | 109 | 110 |
| Hungary | 78 | 294 |
| Yugoslavia | 531 | 847 |
| China (PRC) | 5,033 | 8,512 |
| USSR | 2,767 | 578 |

[1]Millions of dollars, f.a.s.

*Source:* U.S. Foreign Trade Highlights, 1988, U.S. Department of Commerce, passim.

## The Democratization Process

Is democracy alone the answer for economic revival and prosperity? Probably not. Although democracy and capitalism usually co-exist, achieving economic prosperity is an altogether different issue. For example, there are countries like India, Egypt, and Brazil that are democracies but are having chronic and severe economic difficulties. For one reason or another, economic prosperity seems to be elusive to many democratic nations. Instead of prosperity, many LDC democracies are riddled with problems of corruption, inflation, and gross mismanagement of resources. On the other hand, there are successful democracies like the United States, Canada, Australia, and Japan that seem to enjoy economic prosperity consistently for several years. In any event, three things are important preconditions for the democratization process. First, the population should have a high literacy rate so that the citizens can understand their rights and responsibilities in a democracy. Second, there should be respect for individual freedom, private property, and equal justice. Third, perhaps a system something similar to that of the United States that clearly divides the power and holds it in check among the executive, judiciary, and legislative bodies must be established.

## CONCLUSION

Transition to democracy and capitalism will be challenging. People may be enamored initially with the idea but, as time passes, they will realize that to become democratic and also adopt capitalistic ways of life all at the same time is an arduous task—especially for the citizens who were used to the communist type of government where individuals did not have to make any decisions. The transition problem can be threefold. First, the people must "unlearn" the past ways of life, and then learn about the democratization process. They must forget the practices of socialism and change their attitudes about capitalism. Under the socialist form of government, the citizens do not have to compete to get good education, employment, health care, and the like, which are usually provided free by the state, whereas under capitalism one has to compete and be willing to pay to get these services. In other words, one has to work harder to have a decent life under capitalism, and the citizens who were not accustomed to such culture will find it difficult to adapt to a new life under capitalism. Second, it is difficult to persuade the well-entrenched bureaucrats to switch from the socialistic ways of operating the government to democratic ways of doing it overnight. The entire governmental administrative mechanism needs to be overhauled. Third, incentives for acquiring private property, wealth, and income need to be established. Also, procedures to collect taxes by the federal, state, and city governments need to be established. New laws must be developed by the elected members, and these laws must have the majority approval before they are implemented. Similarly, a host of policies and programs in various areas, including items ranging from raising revenues through various taxes (income, sales, excise, customs duties, etc.) to policies and procedures on how to maintain a balanced budget, needs to be freshly established.

The democratization of Eastern Europe did not come, unfortunately, at the most convenient of times. The United States and other Western democracies themselves are in an economic dilemma, trying to balance their internal and external budgets by reducing spending and cutting imports. Also, the demand for help from many countries all at one time limits economic aid. These problems are not unsolvable, however; the former communist bloc countries can help themselves. All bloc countries must quickly learn how the market-driven economies operate. To do that, they must understand the role that marketing plays in the stimulation of rapid economic development. Thus, to achieve rapid economic development, marketing education must be imparted to the public at all levels before any substantial financial assistance is rendered to these countries. Also, the barriers that currently exist preventing marketing productivity must be removed. Countries that are offering financial aid to Eastern Europe must make sure that the citizens of these countries understand the concepts of capitalism, democracy, and marketing thoroughly. These concepts must be explained via education at all levels and in all types of institutions. The fact that these concepts are not necessarily parallel makes them difficult to grasp, to understand that marketing is crucial to economic development. Finally, the burgeoning East European democracies should be cognizant of the fact that democracy is not a free ticket to economic prosperity. This is clearly evident from the experiences of many LDC democracies such as India and Brazil where either high corruption and/or public debt have been the prominent reasons for lack of economic progress. Thus, surely, there are lessons for the Eastern European countries from the experiences of democracies in LDCs, and the extent to which these lessons are learned and applied will determine the extent to which their economic development takes place. Marketing must play a significant role in the economic development, and emphasis should be placed on removing barriers and promoting changes that will allow economic development (Dahringer and Mühlbacher 1991, pp. 79–83).

## NOTE

1. The economic problems of the former USSR (now the CIS) and the USSR's former satellites are similar in their origins. The countries, and their economic situations, appear to be differentiated by their political situations, existing cultures, and when they started to convert to market economies. Yugoslavia, for instance, may be unsalvageable as a single

political entity. Poland, on the other hand, has a solid political identity and started to move to a market economy before the USSR started its formal breakup.

# 5

# An Integrated Macro-Behavioral Model of Development

This chapter introduces a model of the relationship between marketing and economic development. First, an existing model of the Japanese economic miracle is examined, and then marketing is integrated into it.

## BACKGROUND PERSPECTIVES

Economic miracles do not happen by chance. Conscious, resolute, and well-coordinated efforts by individuals in management, government, labor unions, and trade associations are necessary. Marketing can do its best in furthering economic development only when other aspects of the economy facilitate development. Such is the case, on the whole, in the economies of the United States, Japan, other developed countries (DCs), and the Pacific Rim newly industrialized countries (NICs). The commercial history of Japan is especially noteworthy because of its outstanding success and the longevity of that success. The saga of the Japanese economic success continues. It has endured over four decades since World War II. It appears that Japan was and is committed, not just philosophically but also behaviorally, to development. Any nation serious about its own economic development would be well advised to examine the fundamentals of what has happened in Japan; determine what, if any, lessons can be drawn from Japan's experience; and, in any case, emulate Japan's commitment. Except in the most fortuitous and serendipitous situations, economic development in this competitive world cannot be achieved without commitment.

To aid in the examination of Japan and to seek applications of Japan's activities to less developed nations, we have drawn on the previously developed Japanese Economic Miracle Model (Reddy et al. 1984, pp. 40–45) in developing the present model. A model helps us to understand how a set of concepts interact with each other. It is useful if it helps us to better understand how the variables and activities included in a system act, interact, and react to different situations. The present model, focused on economic development, depicts the variables, activities, and interactions that appear to be relevant to development. The model is based on this paradigm: (1) a nation, however resourceless it may be, can develop economically; (2) the behavioral traits of the people can be modified to facilitate development; and (3) a successful blend of necessary behavioral traits with favorable internal and external circumstances can produce a synergistic effect. It has two primary purposes. First, it is intended to be helpful to nations seeking economic development as those nations try to streamline and reset their priorities. Second, it is intended to be helpful to firms doing business with and in those nations by deepening the firms' understanding of the nations needs.

The model, as is the case with all models dealing with complex human and economic situations, is probably incorrect (Campbell and Level 1985). To be "correct" the model would have to include all variables, activities, and interactions affecting the outcome of economic development. This cannot be done, given the present state of knowledge; a "correct" model would include, for instance, all the political and social dynamics extant in the country of interest and all countries interacting with it. It must be understood, therefore, that we are in no way suggesting "the" model to explain the highly complex economic problems of nations. The model is qualitative because there is to date no empirical data relating marketing to economic development. Development of useful empirical data may not be possible because of the great number of qualitative and quantitative variables interacting with each other.

Isolating the most important quantitative variables linking marketing and economic development may not be possible.

### Assumptions

These assumptions were made in the construction of the model:

- The country sincerely seeks to develop its economy.

- The country does not have any reason (political, religious, etc.) to reject marketing out of hand.

- Other market-oriented economies (particularly the United States and other Western nations) are supportive of the country's efforts. The developed countries often feel frustrated by the exploitation of their own markets by the aggressive NICs and Japan and troubled by their own balance of payments and employment problems. They may not react, therefore, as they ordinarily would toward a new country trying to aggressively seek development through export marketing, for instance. One may reasonably expect, however, that the developed countries will not seek to keep the underdeveloped countries underdeveloped.

- The public, bureaucracy, businesspeople, and labor agree that they intend to reach a common goal—economic development.

- Limitations will be taken into account when attempting to operationalize the model. Obstacles to marketing will be seen as limitations.

- Special efforts will be taken to give appropriate consideration to inherent weaknesses such as extreme degrees of corruption, red tape, and bureaucracy.

- Marketing's basic function may not necessarily be the creation of demand in a less developed country (LDC). Rather, it is to satisfy the already existing overwhelming demand for essentials and various other types of goods. In a seller's economy, marketing should be used to smooth distribution and, often, to demarket consumption of luxury goods that the country can ill afford.

- The role of marketing in economic development efforts of the country will develop from the bottom up, by pulling together and making sense of the experiences, insights, and findings reported in studies of the past. It is expected that knowledge in this area is more likely to develop through theory-based field studies than through "armchair-developed grand theories" (Kaynak 1986, p. 94).

- Development plans will contain programs for the development and improvement of marketing systems.

In this effort to integrate marketing into the economic development process of LDCs, the following steps need to be considered fully:

- Despite similarities between marketing systems and the economic development of LDCs, as reported in various studies, there is no evidence to suggest that there are two identical marketing systems in the world.

- It is difficult to predict how a marketing structure will evolve in a country intending to convert its economy into a free-market base. Although the evolution may be expected to be similar to what happened in the West—from production to sales to marketing orientation—the length of time taken to progress may be cut short as countries leapfrog from production to marketing orientations. There is also no reason to assume that evolution will follow the same time schedule in all sectors of the economy.

- Western marketing techniques and institutions can be transferred to LDCs only with attention to the social, economic, technological, and cultural differences between these two types of countries. The transformation of machinery and industrial factories does not necessarily mean that they will be associated with development of marketing techniques and practices, although identical products will be produced by this machinery in any country. Kaynak (1986, p. 96) reaffirms that unless the LDCs show strong evidence that they believe in marketing and what it can do to the economic development process, any discussion of marketing economic development models with them is futile. Also, unless businesspeople in the country recognize that marketing is a specialized managerial function that warrants specialists, it is unlikely that much effort will be made to establish more advanced marketing organizations. Thus, educational efforts concerning the role of marketing and the training of marketing specialists are essential to the future economic development process of the emerging nations.

## Japan's Economic Miracle

The rapid economic ascent of Japan after World War II has been so dramatic that some scholars began to call this phenomenon the "Japanese economic miracle" (Vogel 1981). The rest of the world's business leaders—not to mention the economists and the politicians—continue to be alternately impressed, puzzled, or angered by the extraordinary success of Japan's "economic miracle" and the alert, toughly competitive business society that made it. During the past two decades, Japan's economy has weathered oil shortages, foreign export restrictions, and domestic recessions, and its statistics are business history. In 1960 Japan's $39.1 billion gross national product (GNP) was not quite 8 percent of that of the United States; Japan's $1 trillion GNP in 1980 was almost 40 percent of the United States total. In per capita GNP, Japan will probably pass the United States before 1990. Exports worth $12 billion in 1968 had become $140 billion by 1980 (Gibney 1983). We believe this "economic miracle" may be explained using a parsimonious model that considers attitude, achievement orientation, and adaptability—three behavioral concepts with which most American business executives are familiar. The resulting a priori model may prove to be useful in understanding the issues that might arise when world economies attempt to follow the Japanese economic model indiscriminately (Gibney 1983). For several years, scholars have been writing articles and books on the various facets of Japan: its culture, people, business ingenuity, social norms, management style, and organizational structure of business firms (Baranson 1981, p. 22). Some have attributed the Japanese success to a synergy resulting from a close relationship between Japanese business and government, popularly known as "Japan, Inc." (Rehder 1981). Although the previous writings on Japan have addressed several aspects of the Japanese economy, society, and culture, the present model attempts to integrate the complex Japanese traits into a simplified model. In postulating the model, we may have ignored some major as well as minor points. Because the main purpose is to identify and discuss the most salient Japanese characteristics that are deemed to be the underlying factors for the Japanese economic success, some compromise is necessary.

The model is in two phases. The first phase deals with how Japan has been able to achieve its startling economic successes. The

**Figure 5.1**
**Integrated Macro-Behavioral Model**

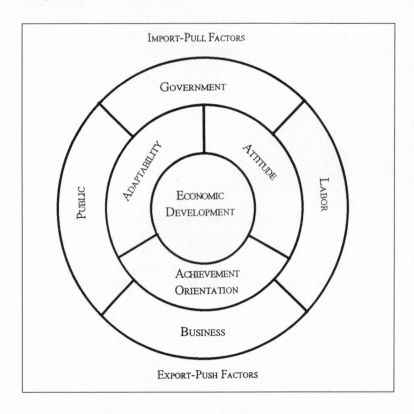

*Source*:  Adapted from "A Macro-Behavioral Model of the Japanese Economic Mir-
        acle," Allan C. Reddy, John E. Oliver, C. P. Rao, and A. L. Addington, *Akron
        Business and Economic Review* (Spring 1984), p. 41.

second phase deals with how marketing and economic development overlay on the Japanese economic miracle model. As background for the postulated model, first let us review two concepts
that have become quite popular. Both Ouchi's Theory Z (1981) and
Pascale and Athos's Seven S's (1981) suggest that the identified
variables contribute greatly to the Japanese economic miracle. The
authors recommend the transfer of Japan's management style to
U.S. corporations in order to improve U.S. economic performance.

## Ouchi's Theory Z

William Ouchi (1981), author of the popular book *Theory Z: How American Business Can Meet the Japanese Challenge*, proposed that the secret to Japanese success is not technology but a special way of managing people, a style that focused on strong company philosophy, a distinct corporate culture, long-range staff development, and consensus decision making. As a result, the Japanese have low employee turnover, increased job commitment, and dramatically higher productivity. Although some American firms, such as IBM, Proctor and Gamble, and Hewlett Packard, can be considered to be attempting to use type Z management, American firms are typically managed by a top-down management philosophy rather than "bottom-up" or "consensus" methods. Also, American management, unlike the Japanese is preoccupied with short-term profits at the expense of long-range market objectives. Theory Z is an attempt to take the best characteristics of the Japanese management style and apply them in United States corporations.

## Pascale and Athos's Seven S's

*The Art of Japanese Management* attributes Japanese managerial success to the use of the Seven S's: strategy, structure, systems, staff, style, skills, and superordinate goals (Pascale and Athos 1981). Although American firms are considered especially strong in the "hardball" S's—strategy, structure, and systems—the Japanese are described as superior in the use of the "soft" S's—staff, style, skills, and superordinate goals. More important, the Japanese excel at integrating all Seven S's. They also focus on creating and maintaining the environment in which the management team works and on making sure that an effective team exists.

## THE INTEGRATED MACRO-BEHAVIORAL MODEL

The model, depicted in Figure 5.1, is behavioral and integrated in character in that it focuses on the critical behavioral characteristics that serve as the catalytic agents for the Japanese economic success: attitude, achievement orientation, and adaptability. These three core variables, constantly interacting and sometimes overlapping, pervade the whole of the Japanese economy. The three core variables are supported by two facilitating environmental factors, "import-pull" and "export-push." A synergistic effect is created by the constant interaction of the core and facilitating factors.

The model integrates various behavioral as well as social and economic factors. An important merit of the model, therefore, is its parsimonious nature. This oversimplification might inhibit its general application, however, especially to countries with sociocultural backgrounds markedly different from Japan's. Nonetheless, the model is likely to be useful to many nations seeking understanding of the nature of the Japanese success. Those countries, after understanding the Japanese precedent, may find that the model is immediately applicable to themselves. Another limitation of the model is that it has not been empirically tested and is based on a synthesis of the currently available literature and opinions expressed by well-known writers in the field.

### Attitudes

An attitude is an overall evaluation that enables one to respond in a consistent manner with respect to a given object or alternative (Engle, Blackwell, and Miniard 1990, p. 46). How do Japanese differ from others? How do their attitudes relate to economic success? What are the related constructs?

The Japanese form a homogeneous society with one language and only two major religions, Shintoism and Buddhism. They are family-oriented and very patriotic; they revere authority, are frugal and hard working, and possess the "Samurai spirit." One notable difference between the Japanese and most other cultures is the intensity with which attitudes are held. For instance, Japanese managers appear to be more pragmatic, warmer, and less moralistic than their U.S., Korean, Australian, and Indian counterparts (England 1975). Japanese managers also attach greater importance to organizational goals, especially high productivity, growth, long-run profit maximization, stability, and industry leadership (Bass 1979). The most relevant personal goals of the managers are achievement and creativity, whereas they express less concern for job satisfaction and dignity in their associations with people. Japanese managers oddly scored low on loyalty, honor, trust, tolerance, and obedience, whereas they placed a high value on aggressiveness (Bass 1979). Perhaps this is because a general lack of aggressiveness in the society makes aggression a scarce and, therefore, highly valued behavior. In his study of twelve national groupings of successful managers, Bass (1979) described the Japanese as wanting to be objective, persistent, proactive, and long term in outlook. Bass also found the Japanese managers to be older, with a slower rate of advancement than managers in the United States, Great Britain, the Netherlands, Belgium, Germany, Austria, Latin America, and India. The Japanese sample rated high on empathy and risk-taking and were more willing to spend more money on product quality. They did not value prestige, security, or pleasure as highly as managers from the other countries, however. The sample also appeared to want cooperation with their peers and were more willing to discuss their feelings with others as well as to tolerate conflict. Their life goals were more apt to include self-realization, leadership, expertness, independence, and duty.

## Achievement Orientation

McClelland and Winter (1969) suggested that a society's orientation toward work and achievement is the major determinant of economic performance. McClelland et al. (1953) described achievers as moderate risk-takers who thrive on innovation and novel situations, as future oriented, and as obtaining satisfaction from immediate feedback that indicates that they have obtained success as a result of their own efforts. Furthermore, McClelland (1962) pointed to achievement motivation as the direct cause of the economic rise and fall of nations. Atkinson (1977), Atkinson and Feather (1966), and Atkinson and Raynor (1974), verified the impact of the achievement motive on individual, or organizational, and national business success.

The Japanese are high achievers, goal oriented, purposeful, and work toward accomplishing their goals through diligence. The literacy rate is almost 100 percent and the society places a high premium on education. Japanese are highly competitive among themselves as well as with the outside world. In almost every industry where Japanese companies have done well in export markets, they have also fought fiercely with each other in their domestic markets. To illustrate, Heenan (1983, p. 43) notes these situations:

- Cameras—at least half a dozen major companies vigorously compete for shares of the domestic market.

- Color televisions—industry leaders must contend with several close runners-up.

- Hi-fi equipment—Technics and Pioneer slug it out with Sansui, Sony, and many others.

- Automobiles—Toyota and Nissan strive for first place with Mitsubishi, Toyo Kogyo (Mazda), and others nipping at the leaders' heels.

### Adaptation

Adaptation is the ability to copy and modify original concepts, product ideas, management concepts, and/or technical know-how. Japan has borrowed extensively from several sources. Many of its manufacturing and management ideas came from the West and were adapted unabashedly to meet Japan's needs. Although its investment in pure and basic research is not comparable to Western levels, Japan has turned to more basic research, in recent years, in selected growth areas, such as information systems and sophisticated communications equipment (Reddy et al. 1984). This new basic research effort will undoubtedly give Japan more tools, more to adapt to its needs.

Japan has outperformed its competitors through meticulous adoption of "the marketing concept," that is, a company philosophy that emphasizes customer orientation as the focal point for a firm's survival and growth. This is well demonstrated by the Japanese automakers' abilities to capture quickly significant market shares in the American and European markets. Japan, as a relative neophyte, holds 30 percent of all small car sales in the United States and thus poses a serious threat to American name plates (Reddy et al. 1984). Japan has also skillfully adopted many other marketing ideas, including segmentation, product positioning, product life cycle theory, and new product development strategies. The Japanese also have been innovative in the adaptation of whatever ideas they have copied. Therefore, Japan deserves to be called an "innovative-adopter." Surprisingly, it has managed to adopt Western production and marketing techniques without disturbing its basic sociocultural fabric. That is why "The Japanese society," says Prime Minister Lee Kuan Yew of Singapore, "is an illustration in Darwinian evolution, the survival of the most resilient social organization" (Heenan 1983).

### Government—Serving the Business Sector

Many scholars suggest that Japan's success is largely attributable to strong bonds and collaboration between Japanese government and business firms (Heenan 1983, pp. 122, 161). Japanese government bureaucrats take it as their serious mission to direct, control, and service various economic activities and policies to achieve economic success for the nation. Hence, the government aids industry in many forms. For instance, the government arranges low-interest financing and guarantees from a variety of quasi-governmental agencies, helps in forming corporate consortia, assures domestic markets, and insures against foreign exchange risks (Heenan 1983, p. 41). Industrial capital in Japan normally comes from banks rather than external capital markets. Because banks obtain their loan money from the government, the latter may exert considerable pressure on the banks whenever necessary. Therefore, unlike American managers, Japanese managers are not too concerned about shareholders and are thus willing to take greater short-term risks, keeping long-term goals in mind (Reddy et al. 1984).

Some of the key government and quasi-governmental agencies are the Ministry of Finance (MOF), the Ministry of International Trade and Industry (MITI), the prime minister's office, the Cabinet, the Diet, and Keidanren (the Federation of Economic Organizations). Government officials in these agencies guide and encourage industries that they expect to become increasingly competitive internationally. Such industries are known as "sunrise" industries. Conversely, they discourage industries that seem unlikely to remain competitive, "sunset" industries. To companies in promising industries, the government grants choice locations of reclaimed land and permission to expand and build new plants. Government creates tax advantages for companies that modernize plants and raises licensing standards to force companies to modernize. Government officials also encourage and assist companies with surplus capital in making foreign investment decisions, establishing insurance systems to provide security for such investments, and negotiating international trade agreements that help rising Japanese industries.

### Japanese Business—Spiritual Goals Dominate over Profit

What are the motivations of Japanese businessmen? What is their guiding philosophy? Japanese business aspirations tend to lean somewhat toward spiritual rather than materialistic goals such as profit. True, profits are required for the survival of a business but profits do not substitute for nonmaterialistic goals such as perpetual maintenance of "harmony" among all parties and peoples. The basis for such Japanese business values and work ethic is the Zen spirit (to be selfless) (Takeuchi 1982, p. 8) and Confucian values that underpin culture and tradition. These, in turn, influence Japanese organizational structures and management systems. Great importance is given to collectivity—the supremacy of the group's rights and goals over the individuals'. Deviators from this norm are punished through social shame or ostracism, which is feared by people more than death in close societies like Japan.

Thus, Japanese business philosophy emphasizes national and company long-term goals more than short-term profits. Against this background, the distinct features of the Japanese managerial system are more-or-less lifetime employment, a seniority-based reward system, and a heavy involvement of management in the lives of the workers, or "industrial paternalism." The Japanese also have a different "Total Quality Management" concept from that of the Western world. It is much broader than in the United States (Berkstresser and Takeuchi 1983, p. 5). Moreover, quality and productivity are regarded as inseparable. Combined with product quality and productivity, the quality of working life forms the foundation of "sound business practices." By comparison, Americans, for instance, regard products or things from the perspective of the Judeo-Christian ethic—things exist for the use of human beings. However, the Japanese perceive products as having their own spirits that need to be respected and cared for.

## Labor—Harmonious Relationship with Management

Labor unions began in Japan with the American occupation of the country after World War II. Although Japan has had its share of costly labor strikes, harmonious relationships between management and labor tend to be the standard. Generally, workers develop a high sense of identity with their firms. This is partly due to the modest differences in cash compensation and visible "perks" between management and workers; workers have no rich capitalist class above them whose lifestyle obviously is dramatically different from theirs. The cooperativeness of unions is best seen in their unquestioned acceptance of modern innovations and the decision of Japanese industries to relocate manufacturing plants abroad even though these actions threaten domestic employment. Because many Japanese firms have profit sharing, the workers get their part of the benefits. Consequently, the Japanese workers believe in innovations and even their firms' compliance with foreign pressures, as long as these actions help their firms to make more profits.

## Public—The Loyal Citizens

The Japanese public has a high sense of loyalty to its nation and will make any sacrifice necessary to put and keep its nation in the front (Reddy et al. 1984). Japan's unique historic, social, economic, and cultural background have made being united to work for a common purpose a necessary survival strategy for the Japanese people. In addition, government, business, and various social organizations continually foster patriotism, common cultural heritage, and values through propaganda, patriotic songs in factories, and other public actions. The following quote from a government communication to the public is an example of governmental activity to foster patriotism (Stone 1969, p. 189):

> Loyalty to the State requires citizens to show love for it in the right way. Indifference to the existence of one's own nation, and disregard for its values, amounts to hatred of one's own nation.

Other admirable characteristics of the Japanese people are their frugality, patience, persistence, diligence, and ability to quickly acquire new skills and adapt them to changing circumstances. In addition to their own characteristics, some other internal and external environmental factors have also contributed to the rapid growth of Japan.

*"Export-push"—an internal environmental factor.* "Export-push" factors are Japanese actions and tactics that have been major catalytic agents in the country's export growth. These factors do not include events or conditions outside of Japan that may have stimulated demand for Japanese products. The major export-push factors are

- building exports through market share objectives,
- adopting the "marketing concept,"
- pricing products competitively,
- providing generous financing terms and conditions to middlemen, and
- designing competitive products.

The Japanese often introduce their products to foreign markets at low prices initially, thereby gaining market share. They are often content to wait for favorable circumstances to make a major effort in a market. For example, the Japanese had to wait until an appropriate time (the oil crisis in the mid-seventies) to gain a substantial American market share for their products. They have been very skillful in using (and still continue to use) the American marketing concept and techniques, "the marketing concept," product design, product positioning, and pricing strategies. The use of pricing and liberal financing terms to dealers and customers have become important tools. If Japanese firms perceive a threat to their present or future market positions, they quickly retaliate by updating or redesigning, product positioning, and keeping a step ahead of their former and would-be challenger(s). This is evident in their present aggressive push in microcomputers.

*"Import-pull"—an external environmental factor.* The "import-pull" factors play an equally significant role in the Japanese economic miracle. These are internal considerations of other nations that produce a conducive environment for Japan to export its products. For instance, the following U.S. market conditions assisted Japanese effort in the United States (Monroe 1978, p. 192):

- changes within the U.S. competitive environment,
- changes in consumer attitudes,
- policy decisions or actions by U.S. firms and government,
- positions taken by U.S. labor that have afforded Japanese producers a better opportunity to gain and hold increased market shares.

Changes within the U.S. competitive environment have come about since World War II when maintaining full employment through increased government spending in order to build aggregate demand became a national objective. With increasing government intervention in the economy, free enterprise and competitive systems have found more and more regulations curbing the freedom of American firms. With government trying to maintain a full-employment policy and easy credit availability compared with other nations, American consumers have tended to indulge in excessive consumption, thus providing vast markets for a variety of products. Product quality and price are the main consumer considerations rather than whether the product is "Made in USA" or made elsewhere.

Another important import-pull factor was (is?) the ever-declining quality of American-made products relative to those from Japan. The decline in quality and workmanship has been attributed to changing values in American life, from hard work to an easy life and saving to spending. Also, it was alleged that the American worker, through union bargaining and over time, became the world's highest paid laborer without a corresponding contribution to an increase in productivity. In addition, there have been several costly labor strikes in the United States, adding to the costs of production and thus making American products noncompetitive either in price or quality with Japanese products. On the other hand, pressured by demanding shareholders who prefer to have their periodic dividends regularly, American management has been in constant pursuit of short-term profits rather than long-range goals. A short-term perspective precludes American firms' competing strategically in international and even domestic markets.

Finally, American government policies in the form of inducements to stimulate new investment or modernize existing production patterns have tended to be either too slow or have not come at all in certain major industries. Ironically, however, the government has provided a growing number of welfare programs to meet certain socioeconomic objectives, hoping to buttress aggregate demand. Although recently Reagan and Bush claimed to attempt to reverse these trends, the effects of the past governmental actions still provide conducive factors for import-pull.

The export-push and import-pull factors work in unison to support Japan's development. Their combined effects can be compared to the actions of the blades of a pair of scissors. Which blade is more important at a point in time can hardly be determined (Monroe 1978, p. 206).

## LIMITATIONS AND CAUTIONS

The model proposed here can be used as a general guide for other nations to examine the Japanese success and to draw from the Japanese experience. It may not, however, be directly applicable to other countries, especially if those countries have sociocultural heritages drastically different from Japan's. Wholehearted adoption of the model by an LDC, for instance, would imply or even require that the LDC's government take a strong and active role in molding the value systems of its citizenry. Any major development is likely to stress the social fabric (Mullin 1991–1992). Should a government place itself in the role of internal propagandist and definer of values? Visions of "Big Brother" abound.

## CONCLUSION

The Japanese have been able to achieve their "economic miracle" not by sheer accident or by blind luck but by setting certain economic goals, doing careful planning, and exercising missionary zeal in achieving the goals. The economic achievements probably would not have been possible, at least in the forty years since World War II, without the active support of the Japanese government. The government played a key role in planning, goal setting, coordinating, and sometimes financially supporting various business ventures that were important to Japanese economic progress. The Japanese government also has been responsible for molding and/or modifying behaviors of the general public, labor, and other concerned bodies in order to support its goals. The interaction of three major Japanese behavioral variables (attitude, achievement orientation, and adaptability) has made the Japanese economic miracle possible. The hard-working Japanese were fortunate to have favorable external circumstances, such as the worldwide import-pull factors (particularly from the market-rich West), and the ability to take advantage of those factors by fostering internal export-push factors. This combination of factors created a synergistic effect that created enormous economic success for Japan, much beyond all expectations.

# 6

# Marketing a Region: The Case of Setúbal

This chapter examines the case of Setúbal, Portugal, south of Lisbon. It shows how marketing in general and the proposed model in particular explain the region's economic development.[1]

## INTRODUCTION

There is another interesting and important aspect of marketing in developing economies—marketing the economy itself to investors. Often this is accomplished simply by developing incentive programs to attract investors to profit and allowing those programs to be public knowledge. Incentive programs may be built around tax havens or holidays, minimizing risk, reducing uncertainties, direct financial assistance, or other inducements. The theory appears to be that investors are actively seeking places and ways to invest and can, by and large, be relied on to discover incentive programs that meet their needs. This chapter examines one such set of incentives, those designed to enhance the economic activity of one region of Portugal, Setúbal, and the results of the incentives. First, the historical background of the European Community (EC), Portugal, and Setúbal are examined. Then the structure of the incentive programs is explained. Because the structure of the programs can be expected to have great impact on their acceptance by interested publics, the structuring is analogous to product design. Finally, the effects of the programs on Setúbal are examined.

## SETÚBAL

Portugal (35,510 square miles on the mainland, 10,300,000 population) is located along the Atlantic coast of the Iberian Peninsula, separated from the rest of Europe by Spain. There are five large cities, a small but growing movement toward suburbanization, and a large rural population. Its location, far more than any other factor, has caused the Portuguese to be of Europe but not part of it (*Diario de Notícias* 1991). It speaks a language that is least understood by fellow Europeans, has resisted participating in twentieth-century European wars, and has tended to look more to the Atlantic Ocean and its former colonies (Brazil, Angola, Mozambique, Goa, etc.) than to Europe for cultural and economic sustenance. One of the oldest republics in the world, it is rich in culture (Schumacher 1987). Its great discoverers dramatically expanded the known world and Portuguese, the fifth most common voice on the planet (*OECD Observer* 1989, *World Fact Book* 1990), is spoken by 164 million people.

The government is unitary and centralized with two levels of jurisdiction: the national level and the municipal level. At the national level, leadership is shared by a president and prime minister. The president has little power beyond a parliamentary veto. Prime ministers are elected by parliament, which is elected by the people. Parliament passes laws but the real political power of the nation lies in the political parties. Members of parliament almost unfailingly vote the position of their respective parties (Opello 1986). The current prime minister is Anibal Cavaco Silva, a member of the Social Democratic Party. On the local level, municipalities retain strong home rule powers. In fact, the national government is attempting to give increasing authority (i.e., local education) to these organizations as it attempts to partially decentralize (Veneza 1986, *Revista Critica de Ciências Sociais* 1988). Perhaps most importantly, the national government has recognized the need for regional governments and is steadily developing new jurisdictions across the country. These are expected to be in place by the year 2000.

The national economy is expanding and shifting from heavy manufacturing and agriculture to light manufacturing and services. At present it is more or less evenly divided among services (45%), industry (35%), and agriculture (20%). What is most significant, however, is that the nation cannot feed itself despite its temperate climate, large land tracts dedicated to farming, and large agricultural labor force; Portugal must import 50 percent of its food (Raven 1988). There are also considerable regional disparities in the quality of life. Greater Porto, Greater Lisbon, and the area between these two cities, the Litoral, are economically expanding and are relatively affluent by European standards (Comissão de Coordenação da Região Centro 1990). The major tourist area in the south, the Algarve, is also expanding but not as rapidly or as completely as the Litoral. The farming regions and areas along the Spanish border (i.e., the Alentejo and Castelo-Branco) are extremely poor and economic conditions are not improving (Kielmas 1989b, Riding 1990a).

**Table 6.1**
**EC Index of Comparative Development**

| # | Category | Rank |
|---|----------|------|
| 1. | Purchasing Power | 12 |
| 2. | Value of Exchange | 12 |
| 3. | Rate of Economic Growth | 1 |
| 4. | Rate of Non-Inflation (Least Inflation = Highest) | 11 |
| 5. | Unemployment Rate | 3 |
| 6. | Number of Autos Per Thousand People | 11 |
| 7. | Number of Telephones Per Thousand People | 12 |
| 8. | Number of Televisions Per Thousand People | 12 |
| 9. | Number of Hospital Rooms Per Thousand People | 12 |
| 10. | Number of Medical Doctors Per Thousand People | 8 |
| 11. | Rate of Healthy Infants (Least Deaths = Highest) | 12 |
| 12. | Expenditures for Education | 12 |
| 13. | Overall Standing in the EC Index | 11 |

Many factors contributed to the slow pace of economic growth. For almost half a century the nation was controlled by an isolationist dictator, Antonio Salazar, and an almost "Kafkaesque" bureaucracy. Under the Salazar regime, there was a strong autarchic economy in which corporatist and syndicalist agreements almost exclusively focused on internal, highly protected markets. The result was that Portuguese industries focused on local markets and stagnated, while "European" industries competed in the world marketplace. Further, the Portuguese were involved in seemingly endless colonial wars in Africa that placed a great burden on the national treasury (Graham 1979).

Largely in reaction to the economic, human rights, and colonial policies of the dictatorship, the Portuguese people successfully organized the relatively bloodless, humanistic 1974 revolution that toppled the regime. The new government immediately moved to withdraw from the colonies. Even peace, however, had an immense cost: The nation was faced with the burden of repatriating 700,000 "Returnados" (Portuguese citizens who were residing in Angola, Mozambique, and other colonies). The Portuguese had to house, feed, and provide jobs for an additional 7 percent of its citizens within the two-year time period of 1974 and 1975 (Downes 1979). All of this occurred while the nation was still recovering from the turmoil of the revolution. It is easy to understand why there were sixteen governments over the next fifteen years (Cody 1987; Delany 1987; Kielmas 1989a; Riding 1990c). Finally, in 1985, with the election of President Soares and Prime Minister Silva, governmental stability returned to the Portuguese people (Riding 1990b).

The economic problems facing Portugal are immense. As Table 6.1 indicates, Portugal ranks last in eight of the thirteen categories developed by the EC to assess the comparative strengths and weaknesses of its member states. Portugal's two highest positions, the rate of economic growth and the unemployment rate, are due largely to the massive infusion of EC funds that are scheduled to be phased out by the mid-1990s. Thus, the figures are distorted. The most informative figure in the chart relates to Portugal's standing in the EC Index of a Nation's State of Development: Portugal ranks eleventh out of twelve (Fernandes 1989).

Under such conditions, it is little wonder that the EC was willing to assist in the financing of the nation's industrial restructuring. The European Community is an organization that most North Americans can identify only as a distant economic abstraction, similar to the International Monetary Fund, the World Bank, and the General Agreement of Tariffs and Trade (GATT). Although North Americans know these organizations are important, the organizations' activities are generally seen as too far removed to directly impact Americans' day-to-day business and private lives. However, the EC, unlike the other organizations noted above, is likely to have a steady, long-term impact on the North American economies and virtually every major community with them. The formation of the EC represents a major step toward the economic integration of twelve Western European nations and the development of a unified market to compete more efficiently with Japan and North America (Sington 1988). The EC planned to fully integrate by 1993 and thereby form the world's largest market, surpassing even those of the United States and Japan. Delays have been encountered; complete political and economic integration may never be achieved. Nonetheless, the European countries continue to move toward market integration. Market integration, in the EC context, means not only that trade barriers between countries will cease to operate but that the term "domestic market" will be synonymous with "European market." Goods, services, labor, and capital will be free to flow without hinderance anywhere within the EC. Virtually all significant trade barriers among the twelve nations will be removed. At the same time, restrictive trade barriers with Japan, the United States, and other nonmember nations will remain. Even if European political integration in the U.S. model is never achieved, Europe is undoubtedly moving in the direction of a "Commercially United States of Europe." This move could cause severe problems for some member countries. Ireland, Greece, Portugal, and Spain are generally recognized as the economically least developed EC members. Can their economies reasonably be expected to compete with the financially strong, technologically sophisticated, dynamic economies of the northern European countries? Probably not. The members of the EC have recognized that, if all nonintegrative factors were simply removed, the less developed countries would fall farther behind and would become more and more impoverished, at least for the foreseeable future. This outcome would not be acceptable for at least two reasons. First, it is not politically feasible. The poorer member nations would fight such an outcome and would hinder integration. Second, the more developed countries recognize that developed countries make better trading partners. Enlightened self-interest requires that the poorer countries be made more prosperous. Over the past few years the EC, then, has been actively working to restructure the economies of these less developed members with the intent of creating a modern economic system in each nation capable of competing in the twenty-first century. In other words, it is a goal of the EC to assist these nations to reach a level of economic prosperity and stability such that it will be able to effectively hold its own within the EC and the world marketplace (Greenhouse 1990). Critical elements of the EC program include infrastructure modernization, labor force skill enhancement, and improved financial incentives to private sector industrialists (as opposed to nationalized firms) to upgrade their operations.

The vehicle employed by the EC to bring change to Setúbal is the Structural Funds Program (SFP). The SFP focuses on five goals for the participating member nations:

- To stimulate economic growth in regions where the economies are underdeveloped.
- To revitalize industrial regions that are in decline.
- To combat long-term unemployment and underemployment.
- To facilitate the creation of new jobs.
- To modernize agricultural practices.

In one way or another, these goals affect local planning activities and directly impact the quality of life wherever the programs are applied. They can be focused directly on specific, selected regions where problems are particularly acute. Portugal, especially in certain regions, is in desperate need of development and modernization. The EC and Portugal have taken a number of specific and cooperative steps to foster Portugal's development by encouraging private investment.

## Legislation

Portugal, like many underdeveloped nations, had placed a number of restrictions on foreigners' commercial activities but has been trying to set its own house in order by recasting its laws to permit and encourage investment. One of Portugal's most important trends is its movement toward granting the non-Portuguese the same commercial and investment rights as Portuguese citizens. For instance, foreigners were prohibited from entering a broad range of industries and the majority of the capital and the management positions of each firm had to be held by Portuguese citizens. The Treaty of Rome, the foundation of the EC, forbids such restrictions vis-à-vis citizens of EC members. Portugal modified its laws to reflect the treaty's terms and took its liberalization process one major step further by granting the same rights to all foreigners, regardless of citizenship, and removed almost all citizenship requirements from business. There are now only four restrictions: foreigners cannot control, except on short-term contracts, enterprises that (1) relate to the exercise of public authority; (2) affect public order, security, or health; (3) relate to production or trade in arms, munitions, or war material; or (4) are based on nonrenewable Portuguese public assets (Decree-Law Nr. 214/86). Rural land ownership by nonresidents also had been severely restricted or, in many cases, prohibited. Many of those restrictions have also been removed. Subject to restrictions on the use of land, nonresidents now may purchase up to 5,000 square meters of rural land and two purchases per household are permitted (Decree-Law Nr. 38/86). Any major liberalization of legal restrictions would be expected to give rise to a great deal of confusion. Portugal recognized this and a process was designed to "maximize the positive effects of foreign investment in Portugal, without any unnecessary interference in the decision-making procedures of companies." Care was taken that investors would be permitted to "know their rights and obligations, without difficulty" (Decree-Law Nr. 197–D/86). The system of foreign investment contracts also was clarified and codified so that all parties would be able to determine a priori what would be expected, vis-à-vis the government, of participants (Regulatory Decree Nr. 24/86) (ICEP 1991). Other liberalization measures frequently are reported in the business press (*Wall Street Journal* 1992a, 1992b). In addition, a series of proactive investment programs were begun.

**Incentive Programs**

A system of programs, designed to encourage and/or channel domestic and foreign investment, was put into place. The following discussion of those programs is by no means complete but is meant to be an overview. It is not, because programs change in response to changed conditions, overly burdened by detail. Some of the funds for the various programs originate within Portugal and some from the EC. The sources of the requisite funds, however, are not usually relevant to the business considering expansion into Portugal. The point is that the assistance (financial, technical, etc.) is available.

*SINPEDIP* (System of Financial Incentives) is meant to reinforce the technological structure of the country by promoting modernization, efficiency, and quality. This program can contribute as much as $162,000$^2$ or 60 percent of the needed investment for a qualifying project. SINPEDIP was funded by the EC for 480 million ECUs (European Currency Units) between 1988 and 1992. It is expected to continue until the EC judges that Portugal has industrial, financial, and technological bases that would permit it to compete within the EC. Generally speaking, SINPEDIP funds are under the control of Portugal; Portugal decides which projects merit incentives.

*SIBR* (System of Regional Based Incentives) is meant to attract industrial investment to specific areas of Portugal and to create jobs in those areas. These areas are the poorest or least developed of the country and include effectively all the country except the Atlantic coast of Lisbon and northward. SIBR-qualifying projects can receive a maximum cash grant of $1,645,000.

*SIFIT* (System of Financial Incentives of Investments in Tourism) is targeted specifically on the support and enhancement of the tourist industry. It specializes in projects such as tourist accommodations, spas, marinas, and tourist hunting zones. SIFIT can provide grants of 10–30 percent of the needed investment in most of the country and 15-50 percent in certain geographical areas. The maximum grant is $212,000.

*SIPE* (Incentive Scheme for Indigenous Resources) helps investors find and define opportunities in Portugal by paying for feasibility studies, technical assistance, and risk analysis to ease access to capital markets. These types of assistance can be provided without limit; the requesting firm may be required to pay as little as 25 percent of the costs of the studies. SIPE can also provide up to $95,000 in direct financial incentive.

*SIURE* (Incentive Scheme for the Rational Use of Energy) seeks to save energy and reorient the way energy is consumed. Projects that qualify for SIURE tend to be "big ticket" items. Depending on the nature of the energy project, SIURE may award as much as $645,000 to each of the various stages of the project plus a regional component of up to 25 percent of the investment required.

*Other Programs.* There are incentive and assistance programs in still more areas, such as information technology, quality, productivity, and vocational job training. Some incentive programs can be combined and cover up to 100 percent of the investment needed. Additionally, Portugal has created additional incentives to work in coordination with the EC programs. For instance, the country offers corporate tax rate reduction, loan rate reductions for qualifying projects, and tax-free reinvestment of capital gains.

## The Region

Setúbal has been a focal point of extensive EC intervention and has received assistance from virtually all of the EC programs. Setúbal is located approximately twenty-four miles south of Lisbon on a peninsula bordered by the Tagus and Sado rivers. Despite its proximity to Lisbon, it is relatively remote from that city. There is only one bridge that connects the region to Lisbon and it is seemingly at perpetual gridlock (Portugal has increased its automobile registration by 30% over the past decade!) (Bruxelas 1990); the only other connection between Lisbon and Setúbal is a regular, although slow, ferry system. The region has thirteen municipalities, 650,000 people, 1,522 square kilometers, three major ports, and an extensive ganglia of highways and railroads. With Porto, on the coast in the northern part of the country, it historically has been one of the two major centers of mature industry in the nation. Given its location, community character, infrastructure, and labor force, one would have expected the region to be in a prime position to prosper and grow. Through the 1970s and 1980s, however, it experienced a two-decade period of decline that ultimately resulted in extensive unemployment (greater than 20%), labor strife and, not surprisingly, a growing Communist Party movement (Afonso 1990, pp. 1–2). Its industrial base, consisting of such basic industries as steel, shipbuilding, and auto assembly, were publicly owned enterprises hindered by a bloated bureaucracy and controls based on social concerns more than economic rationalization (Esser et al. 1990). Many of these enterprises were established under the Salazar regime and protected under corporatism and syndicalism. After the 1974 Revolution, the new government nationalized 53 percent of all businesses with the result that they became less and less competitive over time (Pottinger 1988). As these companies declined, so did local feeder firms. The effect was a regional depression with many of Setúbal's people existing in miserable living conditions (Dickson 1988). Both the central government and the EC recognized that a healthy Setúbal region was critical to the economic well-being of all of Portugal and that action was required if the nation was to meet its goals for membership and if political stability were to be achieved. Thus, the Portuguese central government created the Integrated Development Operation (IDO) for the Peninsula of Setúbal. Its singular purpose is to revitalize the Region's industrial base (Ministério do Planeamento e da Administração do Território 1990).

### The IDO and the EC

The IDO is budgeted to receive 96 million contos (640 million U.S. dollars) for the 1989–1993 period. Approximately 52 percent of this amount is paid by the EC with the remainder coming from the Portuguese central government. The EC contribution in terms of guidance, direction, and funding has been crucial. In fact, without its participation, it is doubtful that any change would have occurred. The IDO is a commission with a small professional staff and a politically appointed president who reports to both the EC and the central government. Two divisions report to the president: (a) the Industrial Monitoring Division, which includes experts in the areas of local investment, industrial development, environmental protection, transportation, and agriculture/fisheries, and (b) the Public Relations Division, which has the responsibility of interacting with companies interested in locating in Setúbal and coordinating development activities with local authorities (Mil-Homens 1990).

The organization has taken each of the five aforementioned goals and adapted them to the region's problems. The planners first focused on the region's locational and transportation assets; the region is strategically located within Portugal and, perhaps more importantly, is a logical gateway for entry into southern Europe. There are three working ports, a first-rate railroad, a highway system that connects the region to Paris and Madrid, and a trained available work force. Thus, the most fundamental principle of industrial planning was enacted: "Build on the positive aspects of a region's present industrial base." Plans were developed to revitalize the ports so that the region could capture a major share of the distribution market for southern Europe.

The IDO planners also recognized that the nation and region could no longer favorably compete with the Pacific Rim nations in three of Setúbal's traditional areas of high employment: chemicals, steel, and shipbuilding. Existing firms had not reinvested in modern equipment and had not kept current in terms of new production techniques, with the net result that they were consistently losing market share. Given the options of encouraging a massive wholesale revitalization of these industries, downsizing these sectors, and refocusing the region's economic base on light manufacturing, the IDO planners opted for the latter (*Público* 1990). Using EC funds designed for retraining displaced workers and for infrastructure expansion, they quickly began to build new industrial parks and to advertise to international firms that a highly disciplined, adaptive and trained work force was available. The IDO also noted that a link between modern industry and higher education had to be established such that new companies could be nurtured. Thus, it established UNINOVA, an institute operated by the New University of Lisbon designed to assist in the development of new technologies. UNINOVA is focusing its efforts on artificial intelligence, robotics, mesoelectronics, and optoelectronics (*Seminário Económico* 1991).

The IDO realized that the Portuguese education system is the worst in Europe. The average educational attainment level of the Portuguese people is less than the fifth grade and approximately 16 percent of the people are illiterate (Stevenson 1986). Although more than 60 percent of Setúbal's citizens have completed ninth grade and the region's illiteracy rate is only 10 percent (well below the national average), the fact remains that upgrading the local schools is essential. Yet, the IDO planners chose not to actively participate in helping to resolve this problem. They believed that this was an area of national responsibility and that the IDO could best place its emphasis on training the person who is immediately ready to enter the work force or who requires retraining.

Throughout the process of developing the IDO plan, there was extensive discussion concerning how to encourage diversification. The staff knew that Setúbal was already attractive to firms looking for activities that required bulk storage, processing, and a location near a seaport. They also expected that strong ties to universities, a hungry and trainable labor force, and assistance programs for starter industries would help to attract growth industries. Still, they were concerned these efforts were not enough and therefore developed programs to revitalize the cork industry and to stimulate the expansion of tourism facilities. The Setúbal region is a major grower, processor, and exporter, one of Portugal's most significant generators of foreign exchange (Instituto do Comércio Externo de Portugal 1990). Unfortunately most of the cork production is based on nineteenth-century techniques. However, by assisting companies in the purchase of new equipment and protecting the best of the cork lands from industrial development, they hope to maintain and enhance the future of this critical agri-business. The region also has miles of sandy beaches, unpolluted rivers and streams, and beautiful landforms to attract tourists. Few tourists come to the region, however, choosing instead to visit vibrant Lisbon or the quiet elegance of the Algarve. The IDO realized it could provide another economic growth option for the region via resort development, the expansion of hotel/conference facilities, and tourism promotion (Afonso 1990, Appendix III). These strategies are working.

Major private investment has occurred (e.g., Ford, General Motors, and Pfizer Chemical). New high-technology plants are being developed and perhaps most surprisingly, newly downsized mature industries are now reinvesting and becoming competitive (Dickson 1990). Today there is a minimum of social unrest and once again Setúbal is becoming economically healthy. Even the local Communist-led labor union is becoming capitalist: The union purchased a chemical company and is operating it as an employee owned firm. It expects to purchase others (Pottinger 1987).

## Outcomes

In December 1990, the IDO reported a decline in unemployment to under 6 percent, the creation of 100,000 new jobs over the past three years, and expectations of further job growth. The region has attracted 70 percent of its new firms from abroad (Câmara do Comércio Americana em Portugal 1990). Perhaps more significantly, there was a dramatic increase in the development and expansion of Portuguese-owned and -operated firms. The increase in the number of major Portuguese-owned firms was largely fueled by a government decision to denationalize the firms taken over after the 1974 Revolution and to privatize industry as much as possible. More than 30 percent of all new private firms in Setúbal are now owned by Portuguese citizens (*Wall Street Journal* 1989). The IDO also reported that 30 percent of the new firms are working in modern technologies for which current markets exist (e.g., ceramics) and that another 5 percent are working on innovative technologies. What has been most surprising and welcome is that there has been a 4 percent increase in employment in the long-established cork-processing industry and that there is evidence of reinvestment in this mature industry. Although all of the above is extraordinary, the IDO staff point out that their greatest accomplishment has been establishing a feeling of action (Mil-Homens 1990). The Setúbal experience exemplifies, at least for the moment, the power of EC funds when a region commits to change. Yet, one must not get carried away by the results of a narrowly defined, five-year plan. In fact, because of the plan's definition and the speed with which it must be enacted, several problems emerged. First, as Setúbal has expanded, it has attracted workers from Lisbon who must cross the consistently overburdened bridge from Lisbon each day. Although there are proposals to lay railroad tracks on the underside of the bridge and another plan to build a new bridge to the east, neither is expected to be built for a decade (Velez 1990). In other words, although the specific infrastructural improvements required for industry are being met, those of regional significance are lagging. This problem will be further compounded by the fact that Lisbon is expected to increasingly shed its older industries, currently located in aged facilities; many of those industries can be expected to relocate in modern facilities in Setúbal. The full potential of Setúbal as an industrial center may be stymied by its inaccessibility to workers a short distance away.

A second critical problem centers on emerging land use conflicts. Throughout the region, there are new, well-sited industrial parks along major highways. They are often, however, immediately adjacent to the famed cork-producing agricultural lands that have been, and still are, economically important to Portuguese exports. As new Ford, General Motors, and other plants move into Setúbal, there may be a further loss of these lands for cork production with the net result that one of the nation's traditional industries will be threatened. The quest for new development has been so strong and rapid that the impact of the potential changes on land uses have yet to be adequately addressed.

A third critical issue centers on protection of the environment. The seaport of Sines, located in the southeastern part of the Setúbal region, is one of the largest petrochemical ports and processing centers along the Atlantic coast. Constructed during the Salazar regime, the port has suffered years of neglect (Ministério das Obras Publicas, Transportes e Comunicações 1987). Further, at no time have the environmental impacts of the handling and processing of these chemicals been adequately determined. Setúbal is now handling more than 60 percent of the nation's hazardous waste with virtually no sophisticated treatment. Although this is recognized and some corrective actions have been proposed (Portugal's national environmental impact act became law in December 1990), the fact remains that industrial expansion, with concomitant hazardous wastes, is outracing environmental protection (Ministério do Planeamento e da Administração do Território 1989, p. v). It should also be noted that environmental protectionism has been politicized in Portugal with all opposition parties seemingly trying to obtain the moral high ground. On the other hand, the Portuguese government has opted for a "jobs first" platform. For example, the Portuguese government has opposed the development of an activist EC position on the environment because it believes such a position would reduce funds required to improve production (*Wall Street Journal* 1990).

A fourth critical problem is a housing shortage. There is a shortage of roughly 50,000 housing units in Greater Lisbon alone and conditions are becoming worse (Concieção 1991). There are several reasons for the lack of attention to housing paid by the

Caixa Geral de Depúsitos, the nation's major mortgage lender (Ferreira 1990). Rent controls have remained largely fixed at 1950s levels and private entrepreneurs, given the extremely high degree of bureaucratic intervention in housing, would rather invest in commercial or industrial buildings. If there are no major improvements in the transportation network to and from Setúbal for a decade, the industrial base booms as it is expected, and the private sector does not build worker housing or government housing programs are slow to develop, housing prices probably will skyrocket in Setúbal. Over time, this will act as a critical drag on the region's economic growth.

Finally, a fifth critical problem centers on the timing of the industrial revitalization programs. Earlier in this chapter there was a description of the planning framework that calls for an appropriate downward flow from the Great Options Plan and upward flow from local plans that would coalesce at the regional level. Little of this is now formally and comprehensively in place. In effect, the quest to meet EC timetables has resulted in the implementation of an industrial plan before a comprehensive regional plan has been developed. Although one can recognize the need for speed and applaud the extraordinary achievements, there are potentially serious impacts that will have to be addressed if the region is to prosper into the twenty-first century. From a top-down industrial policy perspective, the Setúbal experience depicts a partially successful example, for the moment, of how an industrial policy can be effective. The most important elements of this policy are:

- Common agreement of governmental entities at various levels. The EC, the Portuguese central government, and the Setúbal region are all working from the same plans, policies, rules, and regulations concerning the region's future development.

- Income distribution. It was recognized from the very formation of the EC that the community could not function with a disproportionate number of weak economic partners. It, therefore, provided investment funds for the weaker countries and regions such that they were at least marginally competitive. The EC also provided an extensive time period for these countries and regions to adapt.

- Accountability. The EC does not provide blank-check funds for its assisted countries and regions. There are strict rules and regulations governing each of the EC-approved projects. When the projects are not performing as expected, the EC intervenes to either redirect or stop expenditures.

- The absence of targeting. In most industrial planning efforts, there are inevitably focused efforts to attract one type of industry or another. In the case of Setúbal, the region has chosen a different route and is casting a wide net that ranges from petrochemicals to ceramics and from multinationals to local firms. The approach, given the volatility and uncertainty of world markets, makes sense.

From the perspective of Setúbal, the experience represents an example where a region was "planned upon." However, as noted earlier, there is virtually no local planning tradition in Portugal. Portugal, despite the eradication of Salazaresque edicts and the reforms of the Revolution, is still largely governed by Lisbon and its representatives. Given the poverty of the region and its political unrest (as well as its industrial tradition and prime location) one can understand why the central government undertook efforts to improve the region's quality of life. Still, the fact remains that this region has had little direct participation or decision making in its own destiny.

Finally, no matter how much economic progress is made, Portugal and Setúbal have relinquished a significant part of their patrimony. This is quite disconcerting to culturally sensitive citizens of a country that is the oldest republic in Europe, that valued its autarchic independence for most of this century, and that promised local reforms through a revolution. Indeed, as Marrio Camhis (1991), EC director of regional policy, has noted, the Portuguese fear that they will be the Latin America of Europe. The nation's economic destiny is now in the hands of Brussels and the representatives of governments with whom the Portuguese have been distant; it is required to meet the regulations, standards, goals, and objectives imposed by foreign authorities.

There is a high likelihood of increased prosperity, and the Portuguese people are likely to continue to have an improved quality of life. Sometime in the future, however, the Portuguese will have to compete without EC subsidies. When this happens, will Portugal be prepared? There is, in fact, great concern at the highest levels of government that the nation is not moving rapidly enough to confront its new obligations. Will there be a day of reckoning? For example, if German industry outproduces local manufacturing, if Greek olives become cheaper than those grown in the Alentejo, if plastic bottle stoppers replace Portuguese cork, and if shipping moves to Antwerp then Portugal, once again, may well be left to its own future. In any event, there will be a loss of the unique Portuguese character and patrimony. Clearly, entry into the EC has been made at great cost. Equally as clearly, the Portuguese know they have made a pact with people and nations quite different from themselves.

## IN THE CONTEXT OF MARKETING

Examined in the context of marketing, the Setúbal experience shows what can be done to encourage economic development. First, the objectives for the region were decided on by all the major players. A coherent, coordinated plan was conceived. Four necessary origins of the needed resources were identified: governments, investors, political organizations, and individuals. The leaders recognized that each actor (firm or individual) acts in what is perceived to be its own best interest. The needs of each affected public was addressed. Extra-Portuguese governments wanted the EC to prosper; for-profit firms wanted profit; political parties wanted power; individuals wanted better lives. Leaders actively provided information to show each public that its goals would probably be achievable under the new concept of operations and that the failure to make the plan work would almost surely result in a failed EC and greater Portuguese poverty.

Although the development of Setúbal was not formally structured around marketing's traditional four P's, the topics of the P's were thoroughly covered. *Product:* The incentive programs and the various restructuring of Portuguese laws and commercial customs were designed to allow each participant to achieve its goals even if their achievements were not guaranteed. *Promotion:* Information flows were intended to, and were apparently successful at, ensuring that enough prospective participants had the information they needed to decide to buy into the plan. *Place:* The program was designed for one particular region even though many of its components are available in other parts of the country. There is no assurance that the same plan would be successful in other regions or countries. Additionally, the importance of physical distribution capabilities were intensively addressed. *Price:* Some of the costs and risks of development were and are financial. These items were identified; participants recognized that they were reasonable and necessary to reach the goals. Other nonfinancial costs, particularly cultural factors, had to be accepted by the populace as a precondition of success. This acceptance would not have been achieved if the citizenry had not been satisfied that the prospective gains were worth the costs of the cultural changes.

## SETÚBAL AND THE INTEGRATED MODEL

The successful and on-going development of the Setúbal region fits the process represented by the integrated behavioral model proposed in Chapter 5.

### Government, Labor, Public, and Business

These four factors, the model's outer ring, had to work harmoniously toward the agreed on goal of development. All had to give up certain things in order to achieve the goal; all were satisfied that the costs were justified by the likelihood of achieving the objective. Any one of them could have sabotaged the effort if it had allowed itself to focus on short-term or "turf" costs. For example, the central government had to surrender an unheard of degree of economic and planning autonomy to the region; the public had to recognize and accept the fact that cherished cultural values were likely to be lost. Business had to accept greater levels of risk from competition and loss of institutional protectionism; labor (individuals and unions) had to accept new and sometimes strange working conditions, training into new and sometimes strange occupations, and the restructuring of traditional and legislated work rules. This all, and more, happened because the next ring of the model allowed and caused the outer ring to act as it did.

## Adaptability, Attitude, and Achievement Orientation

The outer ring provided the legislative and structural tools but tools are useless unless and until they are used creatively and imaginatively. The great majority of the populace accepted the leadership offered by the organizations on the outer ring. More important, however, is that the populace required the leadership to lead the way to development. The citizenry accepted the costs involved once the costs were explained and justified by the leadership. Individual workers showed themselves to be adaptable and achievement oriented. The strong Portuguese work ethic was capitalized on. The population's attitude toward development and hard work was reflected in the directions set by the leadership of the model's outer ring.

## NOTES

1. The senior author of this chapter is John R. Mullin, Department of Landscape Architecture and Regional Planning, University of Massachusetts at Amherst. Major portions were published by Dr. Mullin as "Implementation of Regional Industrial Policies in the EC: A Case Study of Setúbal, Portugal," *Portuguese Studies Review* 1, 2 (Fall–Winter 1991–1992): 44–61. The cooperation of the *Review* is gratefully acknowledged.

2. All dollar figures are approximate and vary with the dollar/escudo exchange rate. The exchange rate tends to run around $1 equals 130 escudos. One conto equals 1,000 escudos.

# 7

# Economic Development
# and India

This chapter shows how the model proposed in Chapter 5 can be applied to less developed countries to foster development. India is used as an example because (1) that country is sorely in need of development and (2) many of its situation's facets are typical of the underdeveloped but more or less democratic world.[1] First, a short overview of India is presented. India then is examined in the context of the model and suggestions for steps to foster economic development are made.

## INDIA'S ECONOMY—A BRIEF BACKGROUND

India's economy is a mixture of traditional village farming and handicrafts, modern agriculture, old and new branches of industry, and a horde of support services. It displays both the entrepreneurial skills and drives of capitalist systems and the widespread government intervention of socialist systems. Economic growth of 4 to 5 percent annually in the 1990s has softened the impact of population growth on unemployment, social unrest, and the environment. Industry has benefitted from a partial liberalization of government controls. The growth rate of the service sector has been challenged recently by much lower foreign exchange reserves, higher inflation, and a large debt service burden;

the inflation rate was 10 percent in 1992. Its annual industrial production growth rate has been running around 5 percent. The major industries include agriculture, textiles, food processing, steel, machinery, transportation equipment, cement, jute manufacture, mining, petroleum, power, chemicals, pharmaceutical, and electronics. Agriculture accounts for about 30 percent of the gross national product (GNP) and employs 67 percent of the labor force. Principal crops include rice, wheat, oilseeds, cotton, jute, tea, sugarcane, and, potatoes. India has substantial livestock including cattle, buffaloes, sheep, goats, and poultry. The commercial fish catch is about 3 million metric tons per year, placing India among the world's top ten fishing nations. The country has abundant coal—the fourth largest reserves in the world—and minerals such as iron ore, manganese, mica, and bauxite. Major industries include textiles, food processing, and steel. Agricultural output has continued to expand, reflecting greater use of modern farming techniques and improved seed that have helped to make India self-sufficient in food grains and a net agricultural exporter. Tens of millions of villagers, however, particularly in the south, have not benefitted from the Green Revolution and live in poverty.

With 866 million people in 1991, India is the world's most populous democracy and second only to China in world population. It has a little more than one-third the area of the United States. India is quite diverse ethnically, linguistically, and religiously. Its population is 72 percent Indo-Aryan, 25 percent Dravidian, and 3 percent Mongolian and other. Hindi, English, and fourteen separate official languages co-exist with twenty-four other languages spoken by a million or more persons each. India's major religions include Hindu (82.6% of the population), Muslim (11.4%), Christian (2.4%), and Sikh (2%). Since gaining its independence from the United Kindom in 1947, India has been ruled by democratically elected government. The federal government, located in New Delhi, controls the strategic national interests of the country including defense, finance, and foreign policy. State governments maintain law and order, education, and the various state economic development programs. The British legacy in India left a sizable national elite, well educated and committed to principles of parliamentary democracy. The English language links the elites of India's linguistically different regions. India has enjoyed significant domestic and international achievements in the forty years since independence. The nation's territory has been consolidated, and separatist movements in various provinces have been successfully resisted. The federal parliamentary system has proved workable, and the federal government has established its constitutional right to intervene in state affairs under some conditions.

The Indian monetary unit is the rupee. In 1993, one dollar equalled about 33 rupees compared to its 1985 exchange value of 13 rupees per dollar, an erosion of roughly 60 percent in exchange. To promote foreign trade and to speed up economic growth, the government for the first time since the country's independence has made the rupee fully convertible. Due to this convertibility, profits made on investments in India can be repatriated more easily.

In 1990, India's GNP was $254 billion, per capita income reached $300, national income was $34 billion, and national expenditure reached $54 billion. India has consistently incurred annual budget deficits for the last two decades. The reasons for the deficits include its need to purchase oil, capital goods, and technology and the obligation of servicing its foreign debt, defense expenditures, and a myriad of social programs. The deficits are expected to continue for at least the next few years. Increased export earning would undoubtedly help reduce the deficit. In 1990, India's exports totaled $17 billion, consisting primarily of gems and jewelry, engineering goods, clothing, textiles, chemicals, tea, coffee, and fish products. Major export markets are the European Community (EC) (25% of exports), the United States (19%), the USSR and Eastern Europe (17%), and Japan (10%). Imports totaled about $25 billion consisting of petroleum, capital goods, uncut gems and jewelry, chemicals, iron and steel, edible oils from the EC (33% of imports), the Middle East (19%), Japan (10%), the United States (9%), and the USSR and Eastern Europe (8%).

India is a big spender on defense and maintains the second largest army in the world. Ten percent or more of the national budget goes to defense spending, a major burden on the country's meager finances. Its armed forces are well trained, well equipped, and supposedly possess a nuclear capability. India is a member of major international organizations such as the General Agreement of Tariffs and Trade (GATT) and others. Despite its considerable international stature, India has been troubled by disputes with its neighbors and separatist movements inside. India maintains watchful, but generally peaceful, relationships with two unfriendly neighbors, Pakistan and China, but played a leading role in the nonaligned movement. (The fall of the Russian empire has left the nonaligned movement with only one pole to be nonaligned with. It is not yet clear what direction the movement will take.) The Green Revolution of the 1970s made the country self-sufficient in food for the first time since the nineteenth century. The country has a large, well-educated middle class and a growing industrial economy. During 1992, the Rao government attempted to foster economic growth by relaxing the centralized planning controls on international trade and investment that had long stifled the nation's potential.

India faces persistent problems, including separatist movements, regional grievances, and communal conflicts. The benefits of modernization have been unevenly distributed; the majority of the population (65%) is still illiterate and living in rural and urban poverty or near poverty. Corruption is rife in politics and business. Measures to control population growth have been generally unsuccessful. India's historical legacy of diversity and disunity continues to complicate the country's transformation into a modern state.

India provides a poor economic growth model for other developing countries (Cateora 1993, p. 245). Its people are poor, politics are venal, and potential is wasted. Alhough blessed with natural resources, a manufacturing base, and a large domestic market, India lacks vigor in its pursuit of economic development. Although its Asian neighbors have experienced solid economic growth in the last fifteen years, India stayed stagnant. Its indecisiveness and lack of commitment to free trade made India's markets inaccessible to foreign investors and undoubtedly contributed to India's failure to reach its potential.

To encourage foreign investment, India has embarked on new programs liberalizing the economy; elaborate protectionist controls and state monopolies are being abandoned. Public enterprises are being replaced with private enterprise in most areas except defense, mining and petroleum, and railways. Friendly moves toward foreign investors have led to a rush of investment proposals from such firms as IBM, General Motors, General Electric, Coca Cola, and McDonald's. India has the potential to be one of the more prosperous nations provided proper actions are quickly taken. One hopes that India will expand its investment horizons and become part of the economic development boom that until now has passed it by (Cateora 1993, p. 245).

## MAJOR HINDRANCES OF ECONOMIC GROWTH

There are a number of major problems slowing India's economic growth. If they cannot be or are not eliminated, their negative impacts on society need to be softened through legislation, programs, monitoring, and strict application of the law. The hindrances are not limited to economic factors; some noneconomic factors are also important because of their impacts on the nation's mood. Ten of the most important problems hindering India's economic growth are the following.

### Population

Overpopulation is the number one problem of India. India is poised to reach the 1 billion mark in population by the year 2000. Eighty percent of the population lives in villages and the majority are poor.

India does not have a social security system such as those found in the United States and other industrialized nations. Indian children are expected to take care of their parents in their old age. Because male children act as a form of security in the poor's old age, the poor tend to want large families. The poor, then, multiply more rapidly than do the middle class and wealthy. This is rational behavior and the reason for the repeated failure of India's family planning programs. Unlike China where the population growth is strictly supervised and controlled by the communist government, the democratic government in India does not have the political mandate to limit family size. It must be noted, however, that population growth is not by itself a predictor of economic difficulties. If it were, Singapore and Japan would have serious difficulties. To achieve faster economic growth, nonetheless, a solution to the nagging population growth problem must be found and quickly carried out.

## Corruption

Corruption is a cancer that destroys the social, moral, and ethical fabric of a society. In India, as in many other developing countries, corruption in business and government has become a way of life. Unless people, government, and business work together to eradicate corruption, little hope exists for rapid economic growth.

## Religious Conflicts

The diversity of Indian religions presents great opportunities for unscrupulous politicians to exploit differences to satisfy their own goals. People must be alerted to this phenomenon and government must take preemptive measures against this. Otherwise, religious and ethnic conflicts will continue to disrupt society and hinder economic progress. Recent indiscriminate bombings and terrorist actions in major cities like Bombay, Calcutta, and New Delhi make foreign investors and tourists shy away from the country.

## Literacy

Knowledge is power. India's citizens must be able to read and write and understand the democratic process and to be able to compete in an increasingly technological and complex world. India has come a long way since its independence to bring its literacy rate to the current 40 percent. The fact remains, however, that more than 500 million Indians are illiterate. How can this work force compete with, say, Japan where the literacy rate is 100 percent? Compulsory elementary education for all children must be rigorously enforced and adult education programs must also be diligently pursued throughout the country.

## Castes

The caste system is unique to India. India has four major castes and many sub-castes. The four major castes, in order of "rank," are the Brahmins, Ksatriyas, Vysyas, and Sudras. A fifth class, the Untouchables (largely known as Harijans), which comprises 20 percent of the population, historically has been ill treated. Since independence, thanks to Mahatma Gandhi, Harijans get preferential treatment for jobs and college admissions—much to the dislike of the upper castes. There is constant rivalry and suspicion within and between the castes, making the country extremely fragmented in viewpoints, belief systems, and socioeconomic lifestyles. Intercaste marriages are discouraged. Intercaste rivalries and abuse of the lower castes are so common that any "common interest" of the people is difficult to achieve. The Indian population needs to be more educated about the evils of the caste system and ways must be found to motivate ordinary citizens to reject caste considerations.

## Dowry System

India is one of the few countries where parents of female children have to pay dowries to get them married. This practice continues despite being banned by the government. The dowry system is a major threat to the country's economic growth because most people are culturally forced to engage in the pursuit of accumulating money to get their daughters married rather than accept the risk of investing. The dowry system has two serious, sociological and economic outcomes. First, because uninvested money cannot grow, the growth of the middle class is seriously hampered. Second, because the dowry system renders so much money unavailable for investment, the system acts as a very effective damper of economic growth. Until the dowry system is totally abandoned, India's economic advancement will be difficult to achieve.

## Infrastructure

India's current rickety physical infrastructure is largely a by-product of what the British set up to rule the country. Troops and administrators had to move around the country to maintain law and order. Railroads, seaports, airports, and roads were developed with that objective. Since independence, the country has been adding to its infrastructure, but the work is almost uniformly sub-marginal. India's infrastructure, with rare exception, needs massive overhauling and rebuilding. Its highways, railroads, and waterways need to be developed to help accelerate economic growth. In addition, banking, insurance, and various other business service industries must be rapidly established. Ways must be found to maintain both the physical and nonphysical infrastructures.

## Poverty

People living in harsh poverty do not have the "luxuries" of planning and investing. They must feed, clothe, and shelter themselves today; tomorrow is irrelevant. Today, more than 400 million Indians live in poverty. Large numbers of these people must be provided with opportunities to increase their long-term potentials. Low-interest loans, subsidized training facilities, or other potential-enhancing activities would go a long way toward contributing to India's development.

## Judicial System

India follows common law in the manner of the British judiciary system. The judicial system, however, is overloaded and archaic. Case resolution is extremely slow. Civil and criminal cases usually linger in the courts for many years. This problem must be addressed immediately. Conflict naturally arises in business. Domestic and foreign private investors are naturally hesitant to invest in business and industry where legal disputes take forever to be resolved.

## Lack of Friendly Ties with the West

India's past behaviors did not encourage the industrialized Western nations to behave in a particularly friendly way toward the country. India was and is a leader in the "nonaligned" nations movement. That movement, however, was seen by many Western nations to have a definite tilt in favor of the (former) USSR. This may have been a good strategy while the Russian empire existed, but it has left a residue of ill will in the West. Further, India's refusal to sign the nuclear nonproliferation treaty was not well received, particularly in the United States. Changes in the status of the Soviet Union and world politics have created a different environment that should cause India to carefully review its foreign policy positions. More friendly relations with countries important to India's economic development must be cultivated just as Japan and the successful Pacific basin countries are able to do. Those relations should be based on mutual desires. For instance, the people of the United States will probably resent being asked to support programs likely to hurt their own economic well-being.

Aggressive actions must be taken to minimize the negative impact of these hindrances if India is serious about development. In the same manner, other developing countries must clearly identify and aggressively deal with the factors hindering their development. Failure to do so reduces economic development plans to "wish lists."

## APPLICATION OF THE ECONOMIC DEVELOPMENT MODEL

Can India copy the Japanese growth model? India is similar to Japan in many dimensions. For example, Buddhism, which originated in India, spread to Japan via China. There are also similarities with respect to family values, endurance, and resilience common in the Eastern cultures. The similarities may not be as numerous as the similarities between, say, Japan and Korea, but there are definite parallels between Japan and India. Nonetheless, of course, no two countries are alike in every aspect. Japan and India are quite different in many ways. India, for instance, is quite diverse culturally and ethnically, whereas Japan prides itself on being a country with one race, one language, and one culture. The model describes what happened in Japan; we suggest that the model can provide guidance for India's economic development. We suggest that India could most readily achieve economic success by the management of three core elements,

- attitude, achievement, and adaptation, interacting with each other in a favorable environment;
- business, labor, government, and the public, accelerated by two external factors; and
- import-pull and export-push.

### Achievement Orientation

A society's orientation toward work and achievement is a major determinant of economic performance; achievement motivation is a direct cause of the economic rise and fall of nations (McClelland 1962; McClelland and Winter 1969). Since its independence, India has concentrated primarily on public, rather than private, investment and ownership. This has occurred for three primary reasons: fear of exploitation, limitations of Indian private capital, and control of defense industries.

*Fear of exploitation*. Fear of exploitation by private and foreign businesses has been the driving force of India's planners. Perhaps, given the history of the exploitation of India by colonial powers, such fears used to make sense. In today's interconnected, interdependent "global village," however, such fears are no longer rational and are counterproductive. Developed countries and multinational firms recognize, on the whole, that the best trading partners are prosperous. Exploitation, in the long term, does not work.

*Limitations of Indian private capital*. Capital-intensive industries have not been permitted to grow and evolve in India. If India needs a modern communication infrastructure (and it does!), one must be created in toto, starting from, effectively, nothing. This would require a huge and immediate capital investment. Indian business does not have the vast capital needed to establish large iron and steel, telephone and telegraph, and similar big industries simultaneously. Foreign investment, then, is an absolute necessity, and, given the state of the world economy, foreign aid by industrialized countries is unlikely to appear. The American taxpayer, for instance, is likely to say, "Why should I pay for their system? Why not let AT&T do it?" Those questions would be very difficult to answer. AT&T, for instance, can build an Indian communication system but only if AT&T can make a profit by doing so. Private investment is made only in order to make profits.

*Control of defense industries*. The government of India retains control of industries deemed essential for national interests. This is not an unusual situation in the underdeveloped world. It results, however, in the insulation of those "essential" industries from the rigors and benefits of competition. India has taken the concept to the extreme. Arguments can be found to justify designating almost any heavy industry as essential, and India has done so. Thus, governments, both state and federal, own and operate many industries such as steel, aluminum, communications, and railroads. Governments are political entities; they make political decisions. As would be expected, then, government-owned industries are run to achieve political rather than economic ends. India's experiments with public ownership of heavy industries have failed. State-owned firms at the federal and state levels have been, are, and will be net losers. State-owned industries are a drain on the economy. Public employees do not have the motivation to operate as efficiently and productively as employees of privately owned firms. The only comfort is that they provide employment opportunities, a politically useful idea for the party in power. Positive attitudes toward achieving economic growth through domestic and foreign private investment and aggressive export orientation are critical to India's economic prosperity. India must reexamine its definition of "essential" with a bias favoring privatization.

## Attitudes

Attitudes are general predispositions of people toward any object including themselves, the family, the nation, and the world (Reddy et al. 1984). Two general areas of attitudes need to be addressed by India: foreign investment and self-sufficiency.

*Foreign investment.* The long British rule and exploitation of the country by other foreigners before that left the public with a generally suspicious attitude toward foreign investment in India. This attitude can be overcome by educational measures and by example. Members of the public can be convinced that foreign investment would benefit them and examples of beneficial investment pointed out.

*Self-sufficiency.* Most Indians appear to be convinced that government can provide their basic needs and otherwise take care of them. This attitude dampens the individual's drive to succeed on his or her own. This attitude must be overcome. It would be nonrational, however, for the individual to seek self-sufficiency if opportunities to achieve it do not exist. Profit-seeking business activity must be seen as the location in which opportunity lies. Government programs must foster self-sufficiency by providing education and skill training; government policies must encourage private investment and business.

## Adaptation

Can the people of India adapt to Western business concepts? Or can Western concepts of business be adapted to Indian cultural values? Probably, the answer lies somewhere between the two extremes. India has a major advantage over some of its less developed colleagues in that the language of international commerce, English, is found in all walks of Indian life including the legal system. Additionally, there are a number of American-type business schools throughout the country. These schools are meant to be the source of the middle managers so necessary to firms' management. Indian managers, who now are driven by qualities such as perseverance, endurance, and resilience, would be likely to adopt adaptation wholeheartedly if payoffs for the adaptation are available. Adaptation of Western ways of doing business in, for instance, quality control, timeliness, packaging, pricing, distribution, and promotion practices should not be difficult to achieve. Adaptations of Western business ways to the Indian environment can be relied on to evolve if the process is market driven. Well-motivated, rational political and business leadership can stimulate adaptability.

## Government

The state and federal governments own and operate major industries such as iron, steel, communication, and transport. Initially, government ownership was thought of as a process to provide capital and employment and to eliminate the concentration of wealth in a few hands. However, the state-owned and -operated enterprises, with a few exceptions, have turned out to be dens of corruption, inefficiency, and nepotism. Employees lack motivation to produce profits because jobs are permanent. Recently, the government has begun to privatize many public enterprises and is apparently attempting to encourage more private and foreign investment. How can a government change itself to fit the model's requirement? Traditionally, India's government has been anti-private business and pro-public business. But this attitude toward private enterprise is gradually changing as more public enterprises are running into chronic major losses. Public enterprises are becoming recognized as simply unsupportable. India, therefore, has begun a program of privatizing state-owned enterprises. This denationalization program is expected to privatize, eventually, almost all firms controlled by the government. Privatization by itself is not enough. The Indian government must, at least, get out of business's way or, at best, support and encourage business.

## Labor

India has more than its share of strikes and lockouts. One reason is that union leadership tends to be antagonistic to employers. This bias may not have been unreasonable in the past because so many major Indian enterprises have been subsidized or protected by the government. Further, it must be remembered that labor unions are themselves political organizations. Labor leaders must win periodic elections. Too often that is done most easily by satisfying union members that the leaders are fighting an enemy. The "enemy" often is easily identified because family-owned businesses, such as Tatas or Birlas, dominate in India. Responsible labor leaders, on the other hand, recognize that workers in a market economy cannot have jobs unless the firms profit. Union leadership must take a longer view of their members' welfare and use their impressive skills to educate their memberships on the realities of market economies.

## Business

For the reasons outlined above (subsidized or protected industries, political versus economic governmental decision making, family-dominated industries, etc.) Indian business has not had the benefit of competing in a market-driven economy. Without competition, firms allowed themselves to become complacent, bloated, and generally inefficient. Indeed, inefficiency was often encouraged by government, and in many other cases there was little or no penalty for inefficiency. Why would a subsidized firm, for instance, bother to make any investment in efficiency? What payoff would there be? Because efficiency has not been valued in the economy, managers have not learned to provide it. One major problem of Indian business, then, as the move is made to a market-driven economy, is a dearth of middle-level managers. To partly alleviate this problem, firms have their own training programs. In addition, many universities and management institutes have schools of business administration in the pattern of U.S.

business schools. These programs can provide the much-needed middle-management cadre employees. The new middle-management cadre will be able to push for increases in labor productivity through modern personnel, training, and leadership techniques.

### The Public

The population of India is much more diverse than that of Japan. For such a mix of people, unity of mind to achieve an abstract common objective such as economic progress is difficult to establish. It is the responsibility of the government, business, and labor leaders to foster that objective in the population by promoting the idea and its benefits for the country. This objective may be difficult to achieve due to counter-propaganda of vested interests. A political, religious, business, or labor leader can easily use ethnic and cultural differences to exploit the population to its advantage. This threat can only be countered by the other, more responsible leaders.

### Export-Push Factors

Japan, with almost no natural resources, has had to depend on export profits to prosper. Unlike Japan, India has substantial agricultural and mineral resources, which permitted the country not to depend on foreign trade to survive. Mere survival is not the current objective, however. Now the country needs capital for investment for economic development. Export profits can provide the needed capital less expensively than borrowing. Further, World Bank and other loans are getting increasingly difficult to get as more countries vie for them.

What can India export? Historically, India has exported raw material such as jute, tea, gemstones, and so on. Usually, more profits can be made exporting manufactured, value-added goods than raw materials. For instance, India recently has made significant strides in exporting software to the United States and other countries. Companies such as Hewlett-Packard have established bases in India that transmit computer software developed in India to its U.S. headquarters via satellite. India is also fairly well established in the low- to middle-technology engineering-goods global market. Importers of its products include the (former) USSR, Eastern Europe, the Middle East, and Africa. Much remains to be done; India has been much less aggressive than China in its export marketing endeavors. With new export promotion programs and facilities established by the government, India's export marketing is expected to become more competitive in the future. The determination of exactly which value-added products to export should be made by individual, risk-taking investors and firms in the pursuit of profit.

### Import-Pull Factors

Import-pull factors in the West and the United States following World War II have greatly helped Japan to build up its industrial machine. Capitalizing on the demand for imports in other countries, Japan quickly became a mass producer and exporter of quality goods at competitive prices and expert at effectively marketing its goods to the United States and Western countries. Japan's friendly relationship with the United States since World War II has been a great asset in this regard. India cannot benefit from the same friendly relations with the United States and the West due to its fixation with nonaligned countries. Those same nonaligned countries, plus countries that used to be in the Soviet orbit, however, are appropriate export targets. Further, those countries are often less developed also. Surely there is demand in those countries for some value-added products India is capable of making. India cannot neglect, of course, the rich markets of the United States, Europe, and Japan. Relationships must be developed with those countries and their markets must be cultivated and maintained using the same strategy so successfully used by Japan—exporting high quality products at competitive prices. To be able to operate in foreign markets, Indian businesses must improve their marketing skills. The negative image that Indian goods often carry among foreign importers for lack of consistent product quality and timely delivery must be erased through better business practices.

## PROJECTED INDIAN OUTCOMES

India can hasten its economic growth by adapting the economic development model that worked so well for Japan and its newly industrialized Asian neighbors. India's world view needs stability and professionalism (Gonsalves 1993). India needs stability as a matter of law and order. Also, realistic market-driven government policies that will remain paradigmatically stable must be formulated. A generalized administration suited to colonial rule must give way to professionalism. India must realize that there is a greater need for regional cooperation because of the loss of leverage with the rich and powerful resulting from the ending of the Cold War. Unfortunately, many of India's South Asian neighbors' have yet to accept this. Besides regional cooperation with its surrounding neighbors, the gulf countries, and the Southeast Asian nations plus Japan, India must not ignore the prospects of doing business with China and Russia more aggressively. Economic complementarity between India and Russia exists and can be expanded, as is happening between China and Russia.

The need for reform and liberalization and the need to be a player in the global marketplace has been largely accepted as essential for development of the Indian economy. Indian history, like any other, has its cycle of glory and weaknesses. India needs no lessons on human rights and civil liberties. It needs only to live up to the codes laid down by culture and tradition requiring self-discipline, self-regulation, and a commitment to the community and nation. During the 1950s, India played a role far larger than its economic power would have indicated. It later lost its vision and got bogged down in problems at home and abroad. Insecurity was disguised by populism and focusing on past greatness has generated chauvinism.

## CONCLUSION

This chapter focused on India merely as an example. The proposed model can be applied to any number of less developed countries seeking economic development. The key to its application is that all of the model's component parts must be addressed if there is to be a realistic chance of success. It is not enough to deal with each component separately, however. The model must be applied as a coherent whole and synergies among the players must be found.

## NOTE

1. Based on Wright (1993) and CIA (1992).

# 8

# Conclusion

This chapter reviews the book and provides an overview of the model's special properties and applications.

## MARKETING AND DEVELOPMENT

Countries seek economic development to improve their standards of living, security, and stability. As more countries seek economic growth, competition for the world's limited markets and scarce resources will increase. In this challenging environment, only countries with superior marketing skills will be better able to survive, succeed, and develop. Many underdeveloped countries, unfortunately, choose to focus primarily on production. Some even view marketing as a parasitic or wasteful activity and, therefore, are opposed to marketing orientations. These countries, unless they have outrageously good luck, will fail to develop as they should. The failure will have three major results. First, the country's citizens will lead harder lives than they should. The citizenry's best chance to lift itself to a higher plane of material well-being will have been missed. Second, the result of the country's failure to develop will be that its prospective and actual trading partners will be deprived of their own development. The global economy is one, interdependent economy, and economic development is not a zero-sum game. Each country can and should benefit from trade. Those benefits are greatest if its trading partners are prosperous. The third result of a failure to develop is long-term international and/or domestic instability. In this age of global communications, it is not possible to keep one's citizens ignorant of the better living conditions in the market-driven economies of the developed world. When the population of a country is not permitted to better its lot through free-market mechanisms, the population will resent the country's leadership. In such conditions, the leadership can only remain in power by oppressing the people. The oppression could be directly, internally applied. In that case, the population will eventually reject its leaders and the current system. The oppression can be applied by identifying an external enemy and capitalizing on the nationalism of the population. The former USSR used this technique. Unchecked, this technique may result in economic and military chaos.

Japan provides an excellent paradigm for economic development by an underdeveloped country. Japan, after World War II, had almost no capability to support itself. From that point forty-five years ago, Japan has transformed itself into the huge economic powerhouse it is today with $4 trillion in gross national product (GNP), trailing the United States closely. Japan, of course, has had a great deal of assistance in its development, especially from the United States. Nonetheless, Japan's amazing economic turnabout could not have been achieved unless the leaders and population agreed that they wanted it to happen and were willing to make the necessary sacrifices and investments. For instance, Japan's constitution was effectively imposed on the country by the United States after World War II. It only works, however, because the Japanese want it to work. The same is true for many of the cultural changes imposed on Japan. There was nothing to stop the population from recognizing the Emperor as divine regardless of the constitution; they do not choose to.

A thorough study of the Japanese economic and business history led to the development of the model proposed in Chapter 5. The model is based on three sets of variables: (1) attitude, achievement, and adaptation, interacting with each other in a favorable environment of (2) business, labor, government, and the public accelerated by the two external factors of (3) import-pull and export-push. Appropriate marketing skills must be aggressively and consciously developed by less developed countries (LDCs). They must become effective marketers. The first step in becoming an effective marketer is deciding to be one. Entire countries and economies are not, of course, the same as individual firms, so care must be taken not to strain analogies. Nonetheless, a central point about marketers' mind-set can be made by using the response of a successful large firm to its customers as an example. The point is applicable to individual marketers, firm marketers, and country marketers.

Many readers will remember the public uproar that followed the announcement that the formula for Coke was being changed. We recall one of the senior executives of Coca-Cola being interviewed on television shortly after the decision to reintroduce Coke Classic (the original formula "old" Coke) was announced. The gist of the executive's comments were, "Some people are getting a big kick out of this situation. These people think that they are making a great big corporation like Coca-Cola jump around and change its mind because of the reactions of ordinary people. You know something? They are absolutely correct. That is exactly what is happening. Coca-Cola is in business to serve its customers. We will produce the product the customers want." We would add, "And we will promote it, distribute it, and price it so that it meets the customers' approval." The point is that the customer must be the focus of business activities regardless of whether the actor is a firm or a country. The customer is omnipotent. This focus on the customer is the only focus that can lead to success in a market-driven economy.

Some developing countries that have unduly emphasized production at the expense of marketing and, as is the case in India, have become economically stagnant. Such stagnation should be expected *because* exchange activity is not focused on the customer. These countries must introduce or reintroduce marketing into their development plans and become more sensitive to the needs of their domestic and international markets. They must develop pertinent marketing skills and take utmost advantage of the opportunities available to them.

## APPLICATIONS TO COUNTRIES

This book presented the role of marketing in different countries. Marketing's role in the developed countries, the newly industrialized countries (NICs), the former USSR and Eastern Europe, and the LDCs was reviewed. Marketing can be found at different levels of sophistication in each of these groups of countries.

- In the developed countries, marketing is ingrained into the very fabric of society. Even the most economically unsophisticated people assume that they have the right to withhold their business from products and/or suppliers that do not satisfy them. Further, the role of marketing goes beyond consumer satisfaction goals into social marketing goals. Firms see strategic positioning as a major competitive strategy. Marketing research is highly sophisticated. Firms are extremely sensitive to consumer reactions.

- The NICs of Korea and Taiwan consider export marketing as their forte, and they have proven themselves to be masters at it. Their domestic marketing, however, has not yet reached the level of sophistication found in the developed countries. One may expect increased domestic sophistication as those countries continue to evolve. All the major players know from their own observations that marketing works.

- The former USSR and its satellites were opposed to marketing and the assumption that economies should be market driven. They became economic disaster areas and serve as superb examples of the human and economic outcomes that result from planned economies. In these countries, a great deal of groundwork is necessary to educate various publics—bureaucrats, the general public, business, and labor groups—that marketing works. They must all learn basic marketing theory and applications.

- Portugal acted in ways consistent with the Japanese model. The success of the Setúbal project is an example of what can be achieved. Chapter 7 used India as an example of how the model can and should be applied by any number of LDCs seeking development. The LDCs, although they may have some understanding of marketing, have often placed their emphasis on production management. Production know-how often has been considered to be a panacea for economic woes. These countries typically lack marketing vigor in their business efforts and they badly need to develop their marketing skills.

## IMPORTANT FACETS OF THE MODEL

The behavioral growth model used by Japan differs from the conventional economic models because it attributes economic growth more to human behavioral traits than to economic factors. The core elements of the model—attitude, achievement orientation, and adaptability—capitalized on major inherent traits of the Japanese people. Those same traits exist or can be developed in other countries. The core elements interact with each other and operate in conducive public, government, labor, and business environments. These interactions created various synergies that supported tremendous economic growth for Japan. Japan also had other initial advantages—the benefits of the export-push and import-pull factors. Due to scarce internal natural resources Japan had to depend on imports for which it needed the money earned through exports. The same situation exists in many LDCs. Second, following World War II, Japan could help satisfy the tremendous pent-up demand for goods in the United States and the West, and this impetus continues because of Japan's continuing friendly relations with the United States and the West. The same demand for products continues because there is a need in many nations for products that can be produced by LDCs. Korea, Taiwan, Hong Kong, and Singapore have achieved some startlingly rapid economic successes by employing the Japanese model. Malaysia and other neighboring countries are trying to imitate those countries' successes to gain prosperity; it is working.

Perhaps the world would have been more prosperous today had there been proper attention paid to transfer of marketing knowledge along with manufacturing technology. Granted that it is more difficult to transfer marketing skills than production skills, it is unfortunate that somehow marketing so often is an afterthought or even is throttled while production gets top priority. It is important that ways of successfully transferring marketing knowledge and skills be found and the LDCs are helped in achieving their growth objectives. That help cannot be merely money. Throwing money at economically fruitless projects and supporting systems that are other than market driven is not help. Such "help" is wasteful and, in the long term, counterproductive. Both the developed countries (DCs) providing assistance and the LDCs receiving assistance must recognize that the power of marketing is vital for development. Target markets must be selected and vigorously serviced with an effective marketing mix responding to customers' needs. This requires some humility on the part of national and international leaders because those leaders must recognize that they must allow markets to operate. The requisite humility may be hard to find.

Economic success also lies in a country's ability to globally market its products using a high-quality, low-price marketing strategy. Obviously, most underdeveloped countries need export revenues to fuel their economic development programs. Countries like India, blessed with large growing internal markets, also must give appropriate emphasis to their domestic markets. All developing countries must recognize that there are costs to growth. Before a country launches any economic development program, it must identify the major obstacles to growth and take the necessary actions to moderate their negative impact on growth. Whatever specific programs are chosen, marketing is an absolute necessity for long-term economic health.

# References

Afonso, Palhinhas (1990). *The Peninsula Crisis Years of 1984–1985*. Setúbal, Portugal: Desenvolvemento da Península de Setúbal.

Aschauer, David Alan (1987). "Is the Public Capital Stock Too Low?" *Chicago Fed Letter*, Federal Reserve Bank of Chicago (October), p. 1.

———— (1988). "Rx for Productivity: Build Infrastructure." *Chicago Fed Letter*, Federal Reserve Bank of Chicago (September), p. 1.

Atkinson, John W. (1977. "Motivation for Achievement." In *Personality Variables in Social Behavior*, T. Blass (ed.), Hillsdale, N.J.: Erlbaum Associates, pp. 25–108.

Atkinson, John W., and Norman T. Feather (1966). *A Theory of Achievement Motivation*. New York: Wiley.

Atkinson, John W., and Joel O. Raynor (1974). *Motivation and Achievement*. Washington, D.C.: Winston.

Baranson, Jack (1981). *Japanese Challenge to U.S. Industry*. Lexington, Mass.: Lexington Books.

Bartels, R. (1976). "Marketing and Economic Development." In *Macro-Marketing Distributive Processes from a Social Perspective*, edited by C. C. Slater (ed.), Boulder, Colorado: University of Colorado, (August 15-18): 211–217.

Bass, Bernard M. (1979). *Assessment of Managers: An International Comparison*. Riverside, N.J.: The Free Press.

Bennett, Peter D. (1988). *Dictionary of Marketing Terms*. Chicago: American Marketing Association.

Berkstresser III, Gordon A., and Kazuo Takeuchi (1983). *Productivity and Quality: Conceptual Differences Between Japan and America*, Special Pamphlet No. 129. Tokyo: Tokyo Keizai University.

Bruxelas, Maria (1990). Gabinete de Estudos e Planeamento da Administração do Território, December 12, personal interview with J. Mullins.

Câmara do Comércio Americana em Portugal (1990). *Companhias em Portugal com Participação do Capital Americano*. Lisbon.

Camhis, Marrio (1991). "Europe 2000." Speech to the ACSP/AESOP International Planning Conference, July 12, Oxford, England.

Campbell, David P. (1985). "Where the Grass Is Greener: A Critical Review." *International Journal of Comparative Sociology* XXVI (January-April): 122–123.

——— (1987). "An Empirical Examination of Selected Target Firms' Perceptions of U.S. Department of Commerce Export Promotion Programs." Unpublished doctoral dissertation, University of Arkansas.

Campbell, David P. and Dale Level (1985). "A Black-box Model of Communication." *Journal of Business Communication* 22 (Summer): 37–47.

Cateora, Philip (1983). *International Marketing*, 5th ed. Homewood, Ill: Irwin.

——— (1990). *International Marketing*, 7th ed. Homewood, Ill: Irwin.

——— (1993). *International Marketing*, 8th ed. Homewood, Ill.: Irwin.

Certon, Marvin, Alicia Pagano, and Otis Port (1985). *The Future of American Business: The U.S. in World Competition*. New York: McGraw-Hill.

CIA (1992). *World Fact Book, 1991*. Washington, D.C.: Central Intelligence Agency.

Cody, Edward (1987). "Lisbon Seeks End to Volatile Rule." *Washington Post*, June 15, p. A-10.

Comissão de Coordenação da Região Centro (1990). *Plano Regional do Ordenamento do Territóio do Centro Litoral*. Coimbra, Portugal.

Concieção, Carlos (1991). "Mercado de Arrendamento Permanece Estagnado." *Vida Enonómica*, January 11, pp. 4–5.

Cundiff, E. (1982). "A Macromarketing Approach to Economic Development." *Journal of Marketing* 46 (Spring): 14–19.

Dahringer, Lee D., and Hans Mühlbacher (1991). *International Marketing*. New York: Addison-Wesley Publishing.

Delany, Paul (1987). "Buying Binge by Portuguese Fuels Boom but Worries Persist." *New York Times*, September 14, p. D-4.

Dholakia, R. R. (1984). "Missing Links: Marketing and the Newer Theories of Development." In *Marketing in Developing Countries*, G. S. Kindra (ed.). London: Croom Ltd., pp. 57–75.

*Diario de Notícias* [Portugal] (1991). "Portugal tem Lugar Particular na Cooperaçao de CEE com Africa." March 24, p. 3.

Dickson, Tom (1988). "Incentives and Low Costs Lure Investors." *Financial Times* [UK], October 24, p. 3.

———— (1990). "Setúbal Site for Ambitious Park." *Financial Times* [UK], October 24, p. 4.

Djilas, Milovan (1963). *The New Class.* New York: Frederick A. Praeger.

Downes, Charles (1979). *Revolution at the Grass Roots.* Albany: State University of New York Press.

Dreyfuss, Joel (1990). "Getting High Tech Back on Track." *Fortune,* January 1, pp. 74–77.

Drucker, Peter F. (1958). "Marketing and Economic Development." *Journal of Marketing* XXII, 3 (January): 252–259.

———— (1973). *Management: Tasks, Responsibilities, and Practices.* New York: Harper and Row.

El-Sherbini, A. A. (1965). "Marketing and the Industrialization of Underdeveloped Countries." *Journal of Marketing,* 28 (January): 28–32.

———— (1968). "Import-Oriented Marketing Mechanisms." *MSU Business Topics* (Spring): 70–73.

———— (1983). "Behavioral Analysis of the Role of Marketing in Economic Development." *Journal of Macro-Marketing,* Vol. 3, No. 1 (Spring): 76–79.

England, G. W. (1975). *The Manager and His Values: An International Perspective from the United States, Japan, Korea, India, and Australia.* Cambridge, Mass.: Ballinger.

Engle, James F., Roger D. Blackwell, and Paul W. Miniard (1990). *Consumer Behavior,* 6th ed. Chicago: Dryden.

Esser, Klaus, Guido Ashoff, Ansgar Eussner, and Wilhelm Hummen (1990). *Portugal's Industrial Policy in Terms of Accession to the European Community.* Berlin: German Development Institute.

Evans, Joel R., and Barry Berman (1990). *Principles of Marketing,* 4th ed. New York: Macmillan.

Fernandes, António J. (1989). *Portugal Face á Politíca Regional da Communidade Europeia,* Chapter 2. Lisbon: Publica Camões Don Quixote.

Ferreira, Cristina (1990). "Mudanças Seguras." *Público* [Portugal], December 3, p. 13.

Friedman, Milton, and Rose Friedman (1980). *Free to Choose.* New York: Avon.

Gibney, F. (1983). "Japan's Economic Secret." In *Encyclopedia Britannica Book of the Year, 1983,* p. 465.

Gonsalves, Eric (1993). "India's World View Needs Adjustment." *India Abroad,* March 5, p. 2.

Graham, Lawrence (1979). "The Military in Politics." In *Contemporary Portugal, The Revolution and Its Antecedents,* Lawrence Graham and Harry M. Makler (eds.). Austin: University of Texas Press, pp. 221–256.

Greenhouse, Steven (1990). "European Community Leader Watches a Vision Become Real." *New York Times*, January 1, p. 33.

Hayek, Friedrich A. (1976). *The Road to Serfdom*. Chicago: Phoenix Books, University of Chicago Press.

Heenan, David A. (1983). *The Re-industrialization of the United States of America: An Action Agenda for Improving Business, Government and Labor Relations*. Reading, Mass.: Addison-Wesley.

Herrick, Bruce, and Charles P. Kindleberger (1983). *Economic Development*. New York: McGraw-Hill.

ICEP (1991). *Guide for Investors in Portugal*. Lisbon: Portuguese Foreign Trade Institute.

Instituto do Comércio Externo de Portugal (1990). *What Portugal Offers*. Lisbon.

Kahler, Ruel (1983). *International Marketing*, 5th ed. Cincinnati, Ohio: South-Western.

Kaynak, Erdener (1982). *Marketing in the Third World*. New York: Praeger.

——— (1984). "Marketing Research Techniques and Approaches for LDCs." In *Marketing in Developed Countries*, G. S. Kindra (ed.). New York: St. Martin's Press, pp. 238–252.

——— (1986). *Marketing and Economic Development*. New York: Praeger.

Kielmas, Maria (1989a). "Portugal Wants to Sell Off Industries." *Christian Science Monitor*, March 30, p. 9.

——— (1989b). "Portugal's Interior Fights to Improve Economy." *Christian Science Monitor*, April 29, p. 9.

Kindra, G. S. (1984). *Marketing in Developing Countries*. New York: St. Martin's Press.

Kinsey, Joanna (1982). "The Role of Marketing Economic Development." *European Journal of Marketing* 16, 6, 64–77.

Kohler, Ruel (1983). *International Marketing*, 5th ed. Cincinnati, Ohio: South-Western.

Kotler, Philip (1988). *Marketing Management: Analysis, Planning, Implementation, and Control*, 6th ed. Englewood Cliffs, N.J.: Prentice-Hall.

——— (1991). *Marketing Management: Analysis, Planning, Implementation and Control*, 7th ed. Princeton, N.J.: Prentice-Hall.

Larson, Milton R. (1988). "Exporting Private Enterprise to Developing Communist Countries: A Case Study on China." *Columbia Journal of World Business* 23, 1 (Spring): 79–90.

Larson, Paul D. (1989). "Quality Improvement: The Role of Marketing." Paper presented at the American Marketing Association Summer Marketing Educators' Conference.

Leontief, Wassily (1990). "Some Soviet Lessons." *Challenge* 33 (September-October): 14–15.

Levitt, Theodore (1960). "Marketing Myopia." *Harvard Business Review* (July-August): 45–56.

Lovelock, Christopher H. (1991). *Services Marketing*, 2nd ed. Englewood Cliffs, N.J.: Prentice-Hall.

McCarthy, E. Jerome (1971). *Basic Marketing*, 4th Ed. Homewood, Ill.: Irwin.

McClelland, D. C. (1961). *The Achieving Society.* New York: The Free Press.

McClelland, D. C. (1962). "Business Drive and National Achievement." *Harvard Business Review* 40, 4, 99–112.

McClelland, D. C., and D. G. Winter (1969). *Motivating Economic Achievement.* New York: The Free Press.

McConnell, Campbell R., and Stanley L. Brue (1990). *Economics*, 11th Ed. New York: McGraw-Hill.

Mil-Homens, Rui (1990). President of the IDO, personal interview with J. Mullins, December 5.

Ministério das Obras Publicas, Transportes e Comunicações (1987). *O Sector dos Transportes em Portugal*, Lisbon.

Ministério do Planeamento e da Administração do Território (1989). *Relatório Estado do Ambiente e Ordenamento do Território*, Lisbon.

———— (1990). *Operação Integrada de Desenvolvimento da Península de Setúbal*, Lisbon.

Monroe, Kent B. (1976). "The Influence of Price Differences and Brand Familiarity on Brand Preferences." *Journal of Consumer Research* 3, 1 (June): 42–49.

Monroe, Wilbur F. (1978). *Japanese Exports to the U.S.: Analysis of "Import-Pull" and "Export-Pull" Factors.* Washington, D.C.: U.S. Japan Trade Council.

Moyer, R. (1965). "Marketing in Economic Development." *International Business Occasional Paper No. 1.* East Lansing: Michigan State University.

Mullin, John R. (1991–1992). "Implementation of Regional Industrial Policies in the EC: A Case Study of Setúbal, Portugal." *Portuguese Studies Review* 1, 2 (Fall-Winter): 44–61.

*OECD Observer* (1989). No. 159 (August-September): 33–35.

Opello, Walter C., Jr. (1986). "Portugal's Parliament: An Organizational Analysis of Legislative Performance." *Legislative Studies Quarterly* XI, 3 (August): 291–319.

Ouchi, William (1981). *Theory Z: How American Business Can Meet The Japanese Challenge.* Reading, Mass.: Warner Communications Company.

Pascale, R. Tanner, and Anthony G. Athos (1981). *The Art of Japanese Management.* New York: Simon and Schuster.

Pottinger, Ken (1987). "Portuguese Policy Shift Has Lisbon Stock Market in High Gear." *Christian Science Monitor*, February 19, p. 19.

——— (1988). "Who Will Get Profits from Portugal's Return to Private Enterprise?" *Christian Science Monitor*, June 30, p. 16.

Público [Portugal] (1990). "Incubator de Setúbal dá Primeiros Frutos." December 13, p. 36.

Raven, George (1988). "The Development of the Portuguese Agrarian Reform." *Journal of Rural Studies* 4, 1, 35–43.

Reddy, Allan C. (1989). "Marketing and Economic Development: Lessons for Less Developed Countries from Newly Industrialized Countries." *International Journal of Management* 6, 4 (December): 405–411.

Reddy, Allan C., John E. Oliver, C. P. Rao, and A. L. Addington (1984). "A Macro-Behavioral Model of the Japanese Economic Miracle." *Akron Business and Economic Review* 15, 1 (Spring): 40–45.

Reddy, Allan C., L. Wade Humphreys, C. P. Rao, and Ben Oumlil (1992). "A Macromarketing Perspective of the Soviet Union." *International Journal of Management* 9, 3 (September): 247–254.

Rehder, R. R. (1981). "Japan's Synergistic Society: How It Works and Its Implications for the United States." *Management Review* 70, 10, 64–70.

*Revista Crítica de Ciências Sociais* [Portugal] (1988). No. 25/26 (December).

Riding, Alan (1990a). "On Portuguese Farms, a Leftist Dream Withers." *New York Times*, April 20, p. 9.

——— (1990b). "Portuguese Revolution Settles into Stability." *New York Times*, April 29, p. 10.

——— (1990c). "Portugal Is Leaving Its Poor Past Behind." *New York Times*, May 7, pp. 6–7.

Rostow, W. W. (1965). "The Concept of a National Market and Its Economic Growth Implications," In *Marketing and Economic Development*, P. D. Bennett (ed.) Chicago: American Marketing Association, pp. 11–20.

Schumacher, Edward (1987). "Portugal Poor and Unsure of Itself Hesitatingly Looks for a Role in Europe." *New York Times*, March 16, p. A-6.

*Seminário Económico* [Portugal] (1991). "Parques de Ciências Como Instrumentos do Desenvolvimento Local e Regional." January 4.

Sharma, Arun, and Luis V. Dominguez (1992). "Channel Evolution: A Framework for Analysis." *Journal of the Academy of Marketing Science* 20 (Winter): 1–16.

Sington, Phillip (1988). "Lisbon Cashes in on the EC." *Euromoney*, September, p. 115.

Smith, Adam (1937). *The Wealth of Nations*. New York: Random House.

Stevenson, Richard W. (1986). "Johnson & Johnson's Recovery." *New York Times*, July 5, pp. 33, 34.

Stone, Peter B. (1969). *Japan Surges Ahead*. New York: Praeger.

Summers, Lawrence H. (1990). "Soviet Federalism." *Challenge* September-October, pp. 15–16.

Takeuchi, Kazuo (1982). *The Changing Work Ethic of the Japanese.* Special Pamphlet No. 124. Tokyo: Tokyo Economics University.

*U.S. Foreign Trade Highlights, 1988* (1988). Washington, D.C.: U.S. Department of Commerce.

Velez, João P. (1990). "Dinamarqueses Propõem Túnel sob o Rio Tejo." *Público*, December 19, p. 46.

Veneza, Ana (1986). "O Poder Local, 1976–1984." *Revista Critica de Ciências Sociais*, No. 25/26 (February): 693–708.

Vogel, Ezra F. (1981). "The Miracle of Japan." *Saturday Review* 6, 11, 18–23.

*Wall Street Journal* (1989). "Privatization Is a Top Priority." December 19, p. B-9.

———— (1990). "EC Environmental Agency." March 23, p. A-12.

———— (1992a). "World Wire: Portugal Changes Deposit Rule." July 21, p. A-9.

———— (1992b). "World Wire: Portugal to Liberalize Financing." August 7, p. A-6.

Wood, R. Van, and John R. Darling (1993). "The Marketing Challenges of the Newly Independent Republics: Product Competitiveness in Global Markets." *Journal of International Marketing* 1, 1, 77–102.

*World Fact Book* (1990). "Portugal." Washington, D.C.: Central Intelligence Agency, pp. 225–56.

Wright, John W. (ed.) (1993). *The Universal Almanac.* New York: Andrews and McMeel, pp. 406–408.

# Additional Readings

Adams, Walter, and James W. Brock (1986). *The Bigness Complex*. New York: Pantheon Books.

Anderson, Gary M. (1987). "The US Federal Deficit and National Debt: A Political and Economic History." In *Deficits,* James M. Buchannan, Charles K. Rowley, and Robert D. Tollison (eds.), New York: Basil Blackwell, pp. 9–46.

Ansoff, H. Igor (1988). *The New Corporate Strategy*. New York: Wiley.

Arnesen, Peter J. (ed.) (1987). *The Japanese Competition: Phase 2*. Ann Arbor: Center for Japanese Studies, The University of Michigan.

Assael, Henry (1987). *Consumer Behavior and Marketing Action*, 3rd Ed. Boston: PWS-Kent.

*Atlanta Constitution* (1989). "Consumer Trends Change Convenience over Loyalty." September 24, p. R-2.

Bailey, Victor B., Joanne Tucker, and Bruce Guthrie (1989). *U.S. Foreign Trade Highlights 1988*. Washington, D.C.: Office of Trade and Investment Analysis, International Trade Administration, U.S. Department of Commerce, July.

*Banker* [UK] (1987). "Japanese Banks Undercut a Bigger Slice." March, pp. 50–51.

Bell, D. E., R. L. Keeney, and J. D. C. Little (1975). "A Market Share Theorem." *Journal of Marketing Research* XII, 2 (May): 136–141.

Bergsten, C., and William R. Cline (1987). *The United States–Japan Economic Problems*. Washington, D.C.: Institution for International Economics.

Binstock, S. L. (1981). "Americans Express Dissatisfaction with Quality of U.S. Goods." *Quality Progress*, January, p. 13.

Brown, Paul B. (1989). "When Quality Isn't Everything." *Inc.*, June, pp. 119–120.

Brown, Stanley A. (1989). "The I.D.E.A. Show You Must Reach for Excellence." *Marketing News*, November 29, pp. 6–7.

Burton, Daniel F., Jr. (1989). "Economic Realities and Strategic Choices." In *Vision for the 1990s: U.S. Strategy and the Global Economy*. Daniel F. Burton, Jr., Victor Gotbaum, and Felix G. Rohatyn (eds.). Cambridge, Mass.: Ballinger, pp. 3–25.

*Business Week* (1989). "Computers: Japan Comes on Strong." October 23, pp. 104–112.

Buzzell, Robert D., and Frederik D. Wiersema (1981). "Successful Share Building Strategies." *Harvard Business Review* 59, 1 (January-February): 135–144.

Bylinsky, Gene (1989). "Where Japan Will Strike Next." *Fortune*, September 25, pp. 42–52.

Callahan, Robert E. (1982). "Quality Circles: A Program for Productivity through Human Resources Development." In *Management by Japanese Systems*, Sang M. Lee and Gary Schwendiman (eds.). New York: Praeger, pp. 76–110.

Cohen, Stephen D. (1985). *Uneasy Partnership: Competition and Conflict in U.S. Japanese Trade Relations*. Cambridge, Mass.: Ballinger.

Corning, Peter, and Susan Corning (1986). *Winning with Synergy: How America Can Regain the Competitive Edge*. San Francisco: Harper & Row.

Cravens, Donald W., Charles W. Holland, Charles W. Lamb, Jr., and William C. Montcrief III (1988). "Marketing's Role in Product and Service Quality." *Industrial Marketing Management* 17 (November): 285–304.

Damanpur, Faramarz (1988). "The Foreign Banking Invasion." *Bankers Monthly*, May 16, pp. 16–17.

de Bono, Edward (1984). *Tactics: The Art and Science of Success*, Boston, Mass.: Little, Brown and Company.

Deming, Edward (1982). *Quality, Productivity, and Competitive Position*. Cambridge, Mass.: MIT Press.

Duro, Robert, and Bjorn Sandstrom (1987). *The Basic Principles of Marketing Warfare*. New York: Wiley.

Factor, Mallory (1985). "Wall Street Must Choose Between Quality and the Fast Buck." *Wall Street Journal*, April 15, p. 28.

Feenstra, Robert C. (ed.) (1989). *Trade Policies for International Competitiveness*. Chicago: The University of Chicago Press.

Fiegenbaum, A. V. (1977). "Quality and Productivity." *Quality Progress*, November, p. 21.

Fogg, C. Davis (1985). *Diagnostic Marketing*. Reading, Mass.: Addison-Wesley.

Fudd, Leonard M. (1988). *Monitoring the Competition*. New York: Wiley.

Furino, Antonio (ed.) (1988). *Cooperation and Competition in the Global Economy: Issues and Strategies*. Cambridge, Mass.: Ballinger.

Gale, Robert D., and Robert D. Buzzell (1989). "Market Perceived Quality: Key Strategic Concept." *Planning Review* 2 (March/April): 6–15, 48.

Garvin, David A. (1984). "Product Quality: An Important Strategic Weapon." *Business Horizons*, March-April, pp. 40–43.

———— (1987). "Competing on the Eight Dimensions of Quality." *Harvard Business Review* 65 (November-December): 101–109.

Glickman, Norman J., and Douglas P. Woodward (1989). *The New Competitors: How Foreign Investors Are Changing the U.S. Economy*. New York: Basic Books.

Godfrey, Blanton A., and Peter J. Kolesar (1988). "Role of Quality in Achieving World Class Competitiveness." In *Global Competitiveness: Getting the U.S. Back on Track*, Martin K. Starr (ed.), New York: W. W. Norton & Co., pp. 213–238.

Groocock, J. M. (1986). *The Chain of Quality: Market Dominance Through Product Superiority*. New York: Wiley.

Hall, Edward T., and Mildred Reed Hall (1987). *Hidden Differences: Doing Business with the Japanese*. New York: Anchor Press/Doubleday.

Hamel, G., and G. K. Prahalad (1988). "Creating Global Strategic Capability." In *Strategies in Global Competition, Selected Papers from the Prince Bertil Symposium at the Institute of International Business*, Neil Hood and Jan-Erik Vahlne (eds.), Stockholm School of Economics, New York: Croom Helm, pp. 5–39.

Harnac, Jo Ann, and Kathleen C. Brannen (1987). "The What, Where, and Whys of Quality Control Circles." In *Management by Japanese Systems*, Sang M. Lee and Gary Schwendiman, (eds.), New York: Praeger, pp. 67–75.

Harrington, H. J. (1987). *The Improvement Process: How America's Leading Companies Improve Quality*. New York: McGraw-Hill.

Iacocca, Lee, and Sonny Klenfield (1988). *Talking Straight*. New York: Bantam Books.

Ishikawa, Kaoru (1985). *What is Total Quality Control? The Japanese Way*. Englewood Cliffs, N.J.: Prentice-Hall.

Jacobson, Robert, and David A. Aaker (1987). "The Strategic Role of Product Quality." *Journal of Marketing* 51, 4 (October): 31–44.

Juran, J. M. (1981). "Product Quality: A Prescription for the West, Part II: Upper-Management Leadership and Employee Relations." *Management Review* 50 (July) 61.

———— (1988). *Juran on Planning for Quality*. New York: The Free Press.

Kami, Michael J. (1988). *Trigger Points: How to Make Decisions Three Times Faster, Innovate Smarter, and Beat Your Competition by Ten Percent (It Ain't Easy!)*. New York: McGraw-Hill.

Kamm, Thomas (1992). "Argentine 'Miracle.' " *Wall Street Journal*, September 11, p. A-1.

Kotler, Philip, and Ravi Sing (1981). "Marketing Warfare." *Journal of Business Strategy* (Winter): 30–41.

Kotler, Philip, Liam Fahey, and S. Jatusripitak (1985). *The New Competition*. Englewood Cliffs, N.J.: Prentice-Hall.

Krantz, K. Theodore (1989). "How Velcro Got Hooked on Quality." *Harvard Business Review* 67 (September-October): 34–40.

Krishna, E. M., and C. P. Rao (1986). "Is U.S. High Technology High Enough?" *Columbia Journal of World Business* XXI, 2 (Summer): 47–54.

Lambert, Zarrell V. (1970). "Product Perception: An Important Variable in Pricing Strategy." *Journal of Marketing* 34, 4 (October): 68–71.

Lazer, William (1986). "Soviet Marketing Issues: A Content Analysis of *Pravda*." *Journal of Business Research* 14, 2 (April): 117–131.

Levitt, Arthur, Jr., and Gordon C. Stewart (1988). "Can American Business Compete? A Perspective of Midrange Growth Companies." In *Global Competitiveness: Getting the U.S. Back on Track*, Martin K. Starr (ed.)., New York: Norton, pp. 271–278.

Lichenstein, Donald R., and Scot Burton (1989). "The Relationship Between Perceived and Objective Price-Quality." *Journal of Marketing Research* 26, 4 (November): 429–443.

Main, Jeremy (1989). "How to Make Poor Countries Rich." *Fortune*, January 16, p. 101–106.

Malpass, David (1992). "Europeans Should Look West for Advice on Sound Money." *Wall Street Journal*, September 25, p. A9.

March, Robert M (1988). *The Japanese Negotiator*. New York: Kodansha.

McConnell, Douglas J. (1968). "Effect of Pricing on Perception of Product Quality." *Journal of Applied Psychology* 24 (August): 331–334.

McCulloch, Rachel (1985). "Trade Deficits, Industrial Competitiveness, and the Japanese." *California Management Review* 27, 2 (Winter): 140–156.

McGrath, Allan J. (1988). *Market Smarts: Proven Strategies to Outfox and Outflank Your Competition*. New York: Wiley.

Michaelson, Gerald A. (1987). *Winning the Marketing War: A Field Manual for Business Leaders*. Lanham, Md.: Abt Books.

Miller, Richard Lee (1962). "Dr. Weber and the Consumer." *Journal of Marketing* 26, 1 (January): 57–61.

Mitroff, Ian I., Susan A. Mohrman, and Geoffrey Little (1987). *Business NOT as Usual: Rethinking Our Individual, Corporate, and Industrial Strategies for Global Competition*. San Francisco: Jossey-Bass.

Monroe, Wilbur F., and William B. Dodds (1988). "A Research Program for Establishing the Price-Quality Relationship." *Journal of the Academy of Marketing Sciences* 17, 2 (Spring): 151–168.

Nakazawa, Kazuo (1989). "Containing Japan Is Not the Answer." *The Japan Times Weekly*, Overseas edition, September 23, p. 8.

Naor, Jacob (1986). "Towards a Socialist Marketing Concept—The Case of Romania." *Journal of Marketing* 50, 1 (January): 28–39.

NeVaer, Louis E. V., and Steven A. Deck (1989). *The Protectionist Threat to Corporate America: The U.S. Trade Deficit and Management Responses.* New York: Quorum.

Newman, Barry (1992). "The Great Sell-off." *Wall Street Journal*, October 1, p. A1.

Nimgade, Ashok (1989). "American Management as Viewed by International Professionals." *Business Horizons*, November-December, pp. 98–105.

Peters, Tom (1988). *Thriving on Chaos.* New York: Harper & Row.

Peters, Tom, and Robert H. Waterman, Jr. (1982). *In Search of Excellence.* New York: Warner Books.

Philips, L. W., D. R. Chang, and Robert D. Buzzell (1983). "Product Quality, Cost Position, and Business Performance: A Test of Some Key Hypotheses." *Journal of Marketing* 47, 2 (Spring): 26–43.

Quelch, John A., Robert D. Buzzell, and Eric R. Salama (1992). *The Marketing Challenge of 1992.* Reading, Mass: Addison-Wesley.

Rabino, Samuel, and Elva Ellen Hubbard (1984). "The Race of American and Japanese Personal Computer Manufacturers for Dominance of the U.S. Market." *Columbia Journal of World Business* XIX, 3 (Fall): 18–31.

Ram, S. and Jagdish N. Sheth (1989). "Consumer Resistance to Innovations: The Marketing Problem and Its Solutions." *The Journal of Consumer Marketing* 6, 2 (Spring): 5–14.

Rao, Akshay R. and Kent B. Monroe (1989). "The Effect of Price, Brand Name, and Store Name on Buyers' Perceptions of Product Quality: An Integrative Review." *Journal of Marketing Research* 26 (August): 351–357.

Rao, T. R. (1976). "Marketing and Economic Development." *Marketing and Management Digest* 26 (January): 15–18.

Reddy, Jack, and Abe Berger (1983). "Three Essentials of Product Quality." *Harvard Business Review* 61 (July-August): 153–159.

Reich, Robert B. (1990). "Who Is Us?" *Harvard Business Review*, (January-February): 53–64.

Reis, Al, and Jack Trout (1986). *Positioning: The Battle for Your Mind*, 1st ed. revised. New York: McGraw-Hill.

Rhodes, William R. (1992). "Latin Lessons for the Russian Economy." *Wall Street Journal*, September 21, p. A12.

Richardson, Peter R. (1988). *Cost Containment: The Ultimate Advantage*. New York: Free Press.

Rubinfein, Elizabeth (1992). "Russia Offers Privatization Plan Amid Turmoil, Currency Crisis." *Wall Street Journal*, October 2, p. A10.

Ryan, Edward, Jr. (1989). "Has the Marketing Concept Returned to the United States?" *The Journal of Business and Industrial Marketing* 4 (Summer/Fall): 61–63.

Samli, A. C., and J. T. Mentzer (1981). "A Model for Marketing and Economic Development." *Journal of Marketing* 45 (Fall): 91–101.

Savitt, Ronald (1990). "Pre-Aldersonian Antecedents to Macromarketing: Insights from the Textual Literatures." *Journal of the Academy of Marketing Science* 10, 4 (Fall): 293–302.

Schiffman, Leon G., and Leslie Lazar Kanuk (1983). *Consumer Behavior*, 2nd Ed. Englewood Cliffs, N.J.: Prentice-Hall.

Schmenner, Roger W., and Randall L. Cook (1985). "Explaining Productivity Differences in North Carolina Factories." *Journal of Operations Management* (May): 273–289.

Schuller, Robert H., and Paul David Dunn (1985). *The Power of Being Debt Free*. New York: Thomas Nelson Publishers.

Scott, Bruce R. (1989). "Competitiveness: Self-Help for Worsening Problems." *Harvard Business Review* 67 (July-August): 115–121.

Shama, A. (1980). *Marketing in a Slow-Growth Economy*. New York: Praeger.

Shetty, Y. K. (1987). "Product Quality and Competitive Strategy." *Business Horizons*, May-June, pp. 46–52.

Skrentny, Roger (1987). "Japan Takes Detroit for a Ride." *Marketing Communications*, April, pp. 70–76, 86.

Sobel, Robert (1986). *IBM vs. Japan—The Struggle for the Future*. New York: Stein and Day.

Starr, Martin K. (1988). *Global Competitiveness: Getting the U.S. Back on Track*. New York: W. W. Norton & Co.

Steiner, George A. (1979). *Strategic Planning*. New York: The Free Press.

Stevenson, Merril (1988). "School Time." *Economist*, May 28, p. 21.

Tageuchi, Genichi, and Don Clausing (1990). "Robus Quality." *Harvard Business Review* 68 (January-February): 65–75.

Takeuchi, Hirotaka, and John A. Quelch (1983). "Quality Is More than Making a Good Product." *Harvard Business Review* 61 (July-August): 139–145.

Terpstra, Vern, and Bernard L. Simonin (1993). "Strategic Alliances in the Triad: An Exploratory Study." *Journal of International Marketing* 1, 1, 4–25.

Taylor III, Alex (1989). "Here Comes Japan's New Luxury Car." *Fortune*, August 14, pp. 62–66.

Thomas, Robert J. (1989). "Patent Infringement of Innovations by Foreign Competitors: The Role of the U.S. International Trade Commission." *Journal of Marketing* 53, 4 (October): 63–75.

*Time* (1989). "Is Government Dead?" October 23, pp. 28–32.

Tull, Donald S., and Lynn R. Kahle (1990). *Marketing Management.* New York: Macmillan.

Viner, Aron (1988). *The Emerging Power of Japanese Money.* Homewood, Ill.: Dow Jones-Irwin.

Vogel, Ezra F. (1985). *Comeback—Case by Case: Building the Resurgence of American Business.* New York: Simon and Schuster.

Waldman, Raymond J. (1986). *Managed Trade: The New Competition Between Nations.* Cambridge, Mass.: Ballinger.

Weber, William P. (1988). "Manufacturing as a Competitive Strategy." In *Cooperation and Competition in the Global Economy*, Antonio Furino (ed.). Cambridge, Mass.: Ballinger.

Whicker, Marcia Lynn, and Raymond A. Moore (1988). *Making America Competitive: Policies for Global Future.* New York: Praeger.

Yamamura, Kozo (ed.) (1989). *Japanese Investment in the United States: Should We Be Concerned?* Seattle, Wash.: Society for Japanese Studies.

Zeithaml, Valerie A. (1988). "Consumer Perceptions of Price, Quality, and Value: A Means-End Model and Synthesis of Evidence." *Journal of Marketing* 52, 3 (July): 2–22.

# Author Index

# Subject Index

**About the Authors**

ALLAN C. REDDY is Professor of Marketing at Valdosta State University, Valdosta, Georgia. He has published in *International Journal of Management*, *Journal of Applied Business Research*, *Journal of Health Care Marketing*, and other business journals.

DAVID P. CAMPBELL is Associate Professor of Marketing at Valdosta State University. His research has been widely published in such forums as the *Journal of the Academy of Marketing Science*, *Journal of Business and Entrepreneurship*, and several proceedings.